World Economics A

Book Serie
Volume 2

Finance as Warfare

Titles produced by the World Economics Association & College Publications

Piketty's *Capital in the Twenty-First Century*
Edward Fullbrook and Jamie Morgan, eds.

Volume 1
The Economics Curriculum: Towards a Radical reformulation
Maria Alejandra Maki and Jack Reardon, eds.

Volume 2
Finance as Warfare
Michael Hudson

The **World Economics Association (WEA)** was launched on May 16, 2011. Already over 13,000 economists and related scholars have joined. This phenomenal success has come about because the WEA fills a huge gap in the international community of economists – the absence of a professional organization which is truly international and pluralist.

The World Economics Association seeks to increase the relevance, breadth and depth of economic thought. Its key qualities are worldwide membership and governance, and inclusiveness with respect to: (a) the variety of theoretical perspectives; (b) the range of human activities and issues which fall within the broad domain of economics; and (c) the study of the world's diverse economies.

The Association's activities centre on the development, promotion and diffusion of economic research and knowledge and on illuminating their social character.

The WEA publishes books, three open-access journals (*Economic Thought, World Economic Review and Real-World Economics Review*), a bi-monthly newsletter, blogs, holds global online conferences, runs a *Textbook Commentaries Project* and in 2015, launched WEA eBooks - a digital-age, book publishing programme.

www.worldeconomicassociation.org

Finance as Warfare

Michael Hudson

ISBN 978-1-84890-185-8 print
ISBN 978-1-911156-06-2 eBook-Mobi
ISBN 978-1-911156-07-9 eBook-ePub
ISBN 978-1-911156-08-6 eBook-PDF

Published by College Publications on behalf of the World Economics
Association
College Publications
Scientific Director: Dov Gabbay
Managing Director: Jane Spurr

http://www.collegepublications.co.uk

Front cover image – detail from *The Lamb*, 1920, Paul Klee

Cover design by Laraine Welch
Printed by Lightning Source, Milton Keynes, UK

Contents

---

[1] This is a chapter from my forthcoming book by Counterpunch: *Killing the Host: How Financial Parasites and Debt Destroy the Global Economy.* A full version with index also will be published by ISLET later.

[2] This chapter, on the use and abuse of mathematical economics, was published in my book *The Bubble and Beyond.*

About the author

Michael Hudson is Distinguished Research Professor of Economics at the University of Missouri (Kansas City). He has written or edited over ten books on international finance, economic history and the history of economic thought, and is a frequent contributor to Counterpunch, Naked Capitalism and Truthdig, as well as RT TV. His major books are *Super Imperialism* (1972, new edition 2002, translated into Spanish (1973, Dopesa), Japanese (1975, 2nd ed., 2002, Tokuma Shoten) and Chinese (2008, Government Publication and Translation House), and *The Bubble and Beyond: Fictitious Capital, Debt Deflation and Global Crisis* (ISLET, 2012).

CHAPTER 1
Finance as warfare[1]

> To simple people it is indubitable that the nearest cause of
> the enslavement of one class of men by another is money.
> They know that it is possible to cause more trouble with a
> rouble than with a club; it is only political economy that does
> not want to know it. Leo Tolstoy, *What Shall We Do Then?*
> (1886)[2]

The financial sector has the same objective as military conquest: to gain
control of land and basic infrastructure, and collect tribute. To update von
Clausewitz, finance has become war by other means. It is not necessary to
conquer a country or even to own its land, natural resources and
infrastructure, if its economic surplus can be taken financially. What formerly
took blood and arms is now obtained by debt leverage.

The creditor's objective is to obtain wealth by indebting populations and
even governments, and forcing them to pay by relinquishing their property or
its income. Direct ownership is not necessary. Fully as powerful as military
force, debt pressure saves the cost of having to mount an invasion and
suffer casualties. Who needs an expensive occupation against unwilling
hosts when you can obtain assets willingly by financial means – as long as
debt-strapped nations permit bankers and bondholders to dictate their laws
and control their planning and politics?

---

[1] This is a chapter from my forthcoming book by Counterpunch: *Killing the Host: How
Financial Parasites and Debt Destroy the Global Economy*. A full version with index
also will be published by ISLET later.
[2] *Complete Works of Leo Tolstoy,* ed. Leo Wiener, Vol. XVIII [London: 1904], p. 124.

Such financial conquest is less overtly brutal than warfare waged with guns and missiles, but its demographic effect is as lethal. For debt-strapped Greece and Latvia, creditor-imposed austerity has caused falling marriage rates, family formation and birth rates, shortening life spans, and rising suicide rates and emigration.

The financial war to gain the land and/or its rent

The prize to be expropriated always has been the land, the most basic and prestigious form of wealth. For ages, its crops supported citizens who fought in the army and provided labor services. That is why subsistence land traditionally was kept in the hands of citizens for their self-support, not "free" to sell or pledge for debt.

From antiquity until 19th-century Europe and North America, land tenure was the defining requirement for citizenship and voting rights. In order to preserve a free citizenry to man the army and provide corvée labor service, crop rights on land to meet their families' basic needs was difficult to alienate outside of the customary holder's family or clan. (Townhouses and other land could be sold freely.)

Long before coinage came into being, economies functioned on the basis of debts mounting up during the crop season, much like running up a tab at a bar. Agrarian debts to royal collectors, public ale women or private creditors were to be paid at harvest time on the threshing floor. But in time such debt, which initially bound archaic economies together (most transactions were on credit, not "cash sales") became a lever to pry away self-support land (or at least its crop yield). When debtors pledged their land or family members in Mesopotamia c. 1800 BC, it was because they had fallen into arrears on obligations for to royal collectors or private creditors. No loans were necessarily involved, but failure to pay for agricultural inputs, beer or other products.

Initially, unpaid personal debts typically were settled by bondage of the debtor or, more usually, his family members (starting with slave girls) to work off the debt. The arrangement initially was temporary, lasting only until a ruler would proclaim a new Clean Slate to restore the *status quo ante*, an

2

idealized state in which each citizen was free of debt, restored to possession of his own liberty and self-support land. But a characteristic of creditors throughout history has been to stretch the legal envelope and break "free" of communal traditions or law by legal stratagems ("loopholes").

The "original" loophole enabling creditors to take self-support land had to fit into the tradition keeping it within the customary family or clan holding it. As long as the indebted family head was alive, creditors left him in place on the land. The opportunity to become interlopers occurred upon his death. To preserve the "letter" of traditional law by which land-use rights passed to sons, creditors got themselves adopted into the debtor's family as number-one son. These "false adoptions" enabled creditors to end up in possession of much of the citizenry's self-support land.[3] Plutarch describes such sidestepping of sons in Sparta a thousand years later. (Not mentioning wealthy creditors, he used the melodramatic trope of a father disinheriting his "ungrateful" son.)

These disinheritance stratagems pushed society along the transition to modern creditor-oriented law, which makes forfeiture or other alienation of land irreversible. *This quality of being freely alienable and liable to expropriation by creditors is what makes modern property "private."*

Also making modern property "private" is its immunity from public protection of debtors endangered by the loss of their land when harvests failed, preventing personal debts from being paid. To save their land from passing permanently into the hands of creditors, it was normal and even traditionally expected that when a new ruler took the throne he would proclaim a debt amnesty to erase personal debts and restore the *status quo ante* – an idealized world in economic balance. These proclamations restored self-support land to its original holders. Freeing citizens from debt enabled them

---

[3] I summarize this phenomenon in "Reconstructing the Origins of Interest-Bearing Debt and the Logic of Clean Slates," in Michael Hudson and Marc Van De Mieroop, eds., *Debt and Economic Renewal in the Ancient Near East* (CDL Press, 2002):7-58, and also in *Urbanization and Land Ownership in the Ancient Near East* (ed. with Baruch Levine, Cambridge, Mass: Peabody Museum [Harvard] 1999). Jeanette C. Fincke, "Zum Verkauf von Grundesitz in Nuzi," in *Festschrift für Gernot Wilhelm* (ISLET: Dresden 2010) reviews the literature and points out that direct land sales also were developing by c. 1800 BC.

to resume corvée labor for public building projects and to fight in the army instead of being detained as bondservants to private creditors.

Rulers faced an ever-present problem of local headmen, creditors and warlords ignoring royal Clean Slates. From the time of Hammurabi c. 1750 BC to Ammisaduqa a century later, such proclamations became more detailed to close loopholes that creditors devised. But "divine kingship" gave way to creditor/landlord oligarchies in the first millennium BC. Where kings survived, they lost the power to overrule creditor claims. Rural usury leading to the loss of land and liberty, and to depopulation, prompting the prophet Isaiah (Isaiah 5.8) to decry absentee owners assembling vast estates by "joining field to field till no space is left and you live alone in the land." Land ownership became concentrated, turning citizens into renters, clients of large owners or simply fugitives.

A similar dissolution of traditional land tenure occurred in medieval England, and as in antiquity local head-men sought to limit central authority. The Norman conquerors had left cultivators in place to pay tribute, originally in crops. Soon after leading the land grab in 1066, William the Conqueror ordered a census to calculate the crop yield to tax. The resulting compilation, the Domesday Book, was produced in 1086. But six rulers later, King John "Lackland" (1199-1216) proved so rapacious in his levies that the barons rose up in protest. The Magna Carta in 1215 and Revolt of the Barons (1217-19) privatized the land's rent for themselves. Subsequent rulers were obliged to tax the towns and consumers rather than the nobility to pay for their wars and interest on the debts they ran up.

Customary land inheritance was untracked when nobles showed their piety by donating their land to the Knights Templar and Hospitallers or pledged it for debts incurred in the Crusades. The sanctimonious identity of these Church banking orders served to disable customary restrictions against the alienation of land, paving the way for later transfers to more secular bankers.

The 16th to 18th centuries saw land grabbers enclose the Commons by insider dealing and legal stealth as well as by usury. The World Bank is sponsoring a modern Enclosure Movement by promoting land registries in Third World and post-Soviet countries. The Peruvian mining official

Finance as warfare

Hernando de Soto explains the rationale: "In the midst of their own poorest neighborhoods and shantytowns, there are ... trillions of dollars, all ready to be put to use," if only land rights could be borrowed against by being pledged "as collateral for mortgages."[4]

It is the first step toward transferring the land to creditors and future buyers on credit. The absence of property "rights" has a major virtue for these squatters in small villages or urban slums. It means that nobody can dispossess them, because they are protected by custom. Registering their abodes would enable them to borrow to make ends meet – but they could be evicted after they spend their mortgage credit and cannot earn enough to pay the mortgage. What de Soto applauds as "equity extraction" by borrowers ends up with them losing their security.

Reporting on the consequences of creating "secure" property rights for foreclosing creditors, *The Economist* notes that there are "two sides to collateral: enforcing the bank's right to repossess an asset is as important as recognising the owner's right to possess it."[5] Another writer describes anecdotal reports "of problems associated with land titles arising from this move. In Thai villages where the duck pond was common property there is now one person owning it and the rest of the village is excluded; in Cambodia unscrupulous property developers have forced land holders off the land."[6]

---

[4] *The Mystery of Capital: Why Capitalism Triumphs in the West and Fails Everywhere Else* (New York: 2000), pp. 37, 86. As president of the Geneva-based International Council of Copper Exporting Countries, de Soto lobbied to counter national sovereignty over subsoil mineral rights. Mark Ames and Yasha Levine, in "The Extraordinary Pierre Omidyar," NSFWCORP November 15, 2013, Calling him the "Friedrich Hayek of Latin America" claiming "that foreign mining firms should have exclusive rights to gold from traditionally communal Peruvian lands, De Soto came up with a clever end-around idea: giving property title to the masses of Peru's poor living in the vast shanties and shacks in the slums of Lima and cities beyond. ... The point was to align the masses' assumptions about property ownership with those of the banana republic's handful of rich landowning families."

[5] "The mystery of capital deepens: Giving land titles to the poor is no silver bullet," *The Economist*, August 24, 2006.

[6] Raymond Makewell, *The Science of Economics: The Economic Teaching of Leon MacLaren* (London, Shepheard-Walwyn 2013), p. 133.

Finance as warfare

Rome's financial war against government protection of debtor rights

Rome's creditor oligarchies made archaic norms of social balance and equity – royal Clean Slates restoring order – a thing of the past. The Roman legal system made the forfeiture or other alienation of land irreversible, not merely temporary. A free population no longer was militarily necessary as the army was made up largely of citizens who had lost their land fell into clientage and ended up being hired to fight as mercenaries.

A century of social warfare from the murder of the Gracchi in 133 BC to the emergence of Augustus in 29 BC saw the assassination of politicians who sought to protect debtors from losing their land and liberty. While locking in their power at home, the Roman Empire defended creditor rights abroad, especially in Asia Minor. Foreign resistance to Rome's financial privatization had to be not only political and legal, but military (like countries seeking to pull out of America's financial orbit today). The Pontus ruler Mithridates waged three wars against Rome (88-63 BC) in Asia Minor, where Roman *publicani* creditors were devastating economies. The Empire won.

War as the catalyst for national debts

The first recorded example of compound interest is inscribed on the Stele of the Vultures in the 25th century BC, calculating the tribute owed to the Sumerian city of Lagash by neighboring Umma after a fight over their buffer territory. Unpayably high, the unpaid levy led to prolonged future conflict, not unlike the reparations levied by the Allies on Germany after World War I.

Historians find a military origin of coined money in Greece, in the form of booty being melted down and divided among the officers and troops, with a tithe donated to the city-temple. From antiquity down through medieval Europe, wars were viewed as paying propositions yielding loot and tribute. Mesopotamian, classical Greek and Roman temples were adorned with the spoils of war, and coined their bullion in war emergencies to pay mercenaries. The word "money" derives from Rome's Temple of Juno Moneta, where the city minted its first silver and gold coins during its wars with Carthage. It was said that the honking of the temple's geese warned Rome's commander of the impending attack by the Gauls in 390 BC. Hence,

6

Juno's epithet Moneta, from Latin *monera*, "to warn" (also the root of "monster," an omen).

"Money, endless money, is the sinews of war," wrote Cicero in his *Philippics* (43 BC). Not only money, but credit. Venice financed the Crusade against Constantinople in 1204 for a quarter of the loot, which it and other Italians monetized and lent to secular kings to wage their own wars of conquest. This influx of silver and gold from the looting of Constantinople catalyzed the financial sector's rise to power. After 1492 the looting of the New World provided silver and gold to finance the expansion of commerce – and also the increasingly expensive imperial rivalries to carve out new conquests.

Financializing the costs of war led to public debts and the modern bond market. Rulers borrowed to buy cannons and build navies, pay troops, hire mercenaries and support allies. Indeed, warfare became financialized long before industry or real estate. And as in any financialized sector, creditors usually ended up with the winnings. Governments paid interest on their bonds. The word originally meant physical shackles on bondservants, a fitting analogy for the position in which governments found themselves. Or, they paid off war debts by selling land, mines and creating public monopolies to exchange for bonds they had issued.

War debts as the mother of royal monopolies

The Church's banking orders – the Knights Templar and Hospitallers – lent to kings and nobles at the top of the social pyramid, first to embark on the Crusades and then to wage wars backed by the papacy. Being uniquely free from religious censure against gain-seeking – along with the high status of their borrowers – undercut Church doctrine condemning the charging of interest. It was only a short step to legitimize commercial credit, on the ground that this helped unify nations as part of divine order giving each region its own particular role to play in global harmony.

The next step was for bankers to finance military conquest, playing the role that the temples of Athena and Juno Moneta had done in antiquity. Unlike the case in antiquity, royal borrowings were owed to private bankers rather than to public temples, and led to a proliferation of taxes to pay their interest charges – largely to foreigners. Subsequent privatization of credit and banking has made the vast majority of debts owed to private creditors, not public authorities (as in the Bronze Age Near East) with more social interest in restoring economic balance.

Rulers sought to pay their creditors by legalizing Crown trading monopolies and selling them for payment in royal war bonds. The new owners tended to be foreign creditors. This is how the Dutch became major investors in England's Crown monopolies (including the Bank of England, formed in 1694) as international banking became the mother of monopolies: the East and West Indies Companies in Holland, England and France after about 1600, and the South Sea and Mississippi Companies in the 1710s. Remitting their dividends and interest abroad caused a balance-of-payments drain whose monetary effect was like paying tribute to military victors.

The traditional objective of warfare – conquest of the land and natural monopolies to siphon off their rent – remains the objective of today's high finance. The difference is that *rentier* wealth is now obtained more peacefully, while retaining its tributary character. Debt leverage has forced the Ottoman Empire, Latin American and African governments to sell off assets to buyers eager to turn public services into opportunities for rent extraction. Since 2008 a similar strategy of asset grabbing has been used against the "PIIGS": Portugal, Ireland, Italy, Greece and Spain. The idea is to enable privatizers to make money by turning industrial economies into tollbooth opportunities. The idea in today's New Enclosure Movement is to privatize what used to be called the Commons. Russians call it grabitization – privatization by officials and well-connected insiders who view the public sector as the source of enterprises and natural resources to be privatized and financialized.

Novelists and historians have been more willing than economists to recognize this dynamic. Honoré de Balzac quipped in *Le Père Goriot* that behind every family fortune is a great theft, long forgotten or indeed "never been found out, because it was properly executed." But not all such origins are forgotten. A century ago Gustavus Myers' *History of the Great American Fortunes* uncovered how many family fortunes were taken from the public domain by colonial land grants, bribery and insider dealing – and how such fortunes quickly take a financial form.

Having used its wealth to gain enough control over government policy to privatize public assets, the financial sector provides credit for privatizers to buy the right to install tollbooths on hitherto public roads, railroads, airlines and other transport infrastructure, phone and communications systems. The aim is to extract monopoly rent instead of providing basic services freely or at subsidized rates. Financialization means using this rent extraction for debt service.

Avoiding war's financial cost leads to classical liberalism

Gaining monetary bullion by running a trade surplus required competitive pricing of industrial exports. This meant minimizing the cost of labor and its living expenses. Imperial economies that spent vast sums on wars and colonial rivalries found this difficult, because they taxed cities and consumers to pay interest on the debts borrowed to make war. In Book V of *The Wealth of Nations*, Adam Smith describes how each new war loan in England was given a specific dedicated excise tax to pay its interest. By the time of the Seven Years War between the French and British in America (1754-63), such war making and taxing was raising the cost of cost of employment, as did the creation and sale of monopolies. High taxes and prices deterred the development of industry.

The perception that military fighting had become a losing proposition economically led early liberals such as Smith to oppose royal wars, colonization and the taxes levied to pay their costs. The cost of imperial overhead was more than most empires were worth. Smith urged Britain to give the American colonies their independence so as to free it from having to bear the cost of their defense. His contemporary Josiah Tucker described the colonies as "a millstone around the neck of England." It was cheaper to give them political liberty, using credit and investment as more efficient modes of exploitation.

A rising element of cost in the modern world reflects the pricing of basic infrastructure services. Public investment traditionally has sought to minimize such costs. But banking viewed great infrastructure projects such as canal building (capped by the Panama and Suez Canals) and railroads as major credit and investment opportunities to profiteer at the economy's expense. Underwriting fees, speculative gains (often from insider dealings) have been as important as interest charges, while fraud and kleptocracy always have been rife. That is how America's railroad barons, monopolists and trust builders became their nation's power elite a century ago, and how the Soviet Union's oligarchs seized public assets after the neoliberal 1991 "reforms." This is what makes financialization the inverse of classical political economy's value and price theorizing.

Financial avoidance of public taxes and duties

From feudal barons keeping the land's rent for themselves to modern corporate profits paid to bondholders, creditors have broken free of tax liability. Banks now receive most of the rental value of land as mortgage interest, mobilizing a populist argument against property taxes so as to leave more rent available to pay bankers. The situation is reminiscent of Babylonian lenders obtaining the land's crop usufruct while leaving the customary holders liable for the labor duties associated with their land tenure.

Now that land ownership has been democratized – on credit – a majority of most populations (two-thirds in the United States, and over four-fifths in Scandinavia) no longer pay rent to landlords. Instead, homeowners and commercial property investors pay the rental value to bankers as mortgage interest. In the United States, bankers obtain about two-thirds of real estate cash flow, largely by reducing property taxes. *The more the financial sector can reduce the government's tax take, the more rent is available for new buyers to pay interest to banks for loans to buy property.* This explains why the financial sector backs anti-tax "Tea Party" protests.

It is much the same in industry. Financial analysts pore over corporate balance sheets to measure the cash flow over and above the direct cost of production and doing business. This measure is called *ebitda*: earnings before interest, taxes, depreciation and amortization. Owners and their creditors aim to make as much of this income tax exempt by counting interest as a tax-deductible cost of doing business.

Lowering taxes on finance and real estate widens government budget deficits. If bankers also block governments from creating their own money to finance these deficits, the shortfall must be met by public borrowing (unless taxes are raised on labor and industry). At the end of this road, when public debts grow too large to be paid out of shrinking tax revenue, creditors demand that governments balance their budgets by privatizing public assets and enterprises. The effect is to turn the public domain into a vast set of rent-extracting opportunities for banks to finance.

This is the kind of resource grab the IMF and World Bank imposed on Third World debtors for many decades. It is how Carlos Slim obtained Mexico's telephone monopoly to impose exorbitant communication charges on business and the population at large. It can be seen most recently in the demands by the European Union, European Central Bank and IMF (the "troika") to force Greece and Cyprus to pay their foreign debts by selling whatever land, oil and gas rights, ports and infrastructure remain in their public domain. What is privatized will become an opportunity to extract monopoly "tollbooth" rents.

This financialization and rent extraction is quite different from what classical economists defined as "profit" – a gain made by investing in plant and equipment and employing labor to produce goods and services. The financial sector makes its gains via interest, fees, commissions and penalties, and by its privilege of credit creation. Land rent, monopoly rent and interest charges are independent external charges on top of the cost of production.

The role of debt in the war against labor

As labor's wages rose above subsistence levels a century ago, economic futurists depicted a post-industrial leisure economy. Left out of account was that the passport to middle-class status involved going into debt to buy housing and, more recently, to get an education. Democratizing housing, property ownership and education on credit has paved the way for banks to extract interest by lending to personal borrowers. More money is made today by exploiting labor financially and making asset-price gains than by employing labor to make profits by industrial production.

Buying out stockholders with high-interest "junk" bonds as the weapon of choice, financial raiders turn industry into a vehicle for bankers to load down with debt, which they pay by intensifying the exploitation of employees. Corporate raiders seize or downgrade employee pension funds by switching from defined benefit plans (in which workers know how much they will receive when they retire) to "defined contribution plans" in which employees only know how much is to be paid in each month, not what will be left for them after financial managers take their cut.[7] (It is a big cut.) This maneuvering becomes a tactic in class warfare when companies threaten to declare bankruptcy if employees do not renegotiate their pension rights, wage levels and working conditions downward.

The rule of the financial jungle is that big fish eat little fish. Companies use Employee Stock Ownership Plans (ESOPs) to buy up their own stock, enabling managers to cash out their stock options at a higher price. A rule of thumb has long been that about half the ESOPs are wiped out in corporate bankruptcies.[8] After Sam Zell's leveraged buyout of the *Chicago Tribune*. The newspaper's employees were left holding an empty ESOP.

Federal Reserve Chairman Alan Greenspan explained the role of rising personal and mortgage debt in today's evolving class warfare. Under normal conditions unemployment at the relatively low 1997 rate (about 5.4 percent, the same as in the boom years 1967 and 1979) would have led to rising wage levels as employers competed to hire more workers. However, Mr. Greenspan testified, a high rate of unemployment no longer was needed to hold down wages. All that was needed was job insecurity:

---

[7] In 1979, 28 percent of American workers were beneficiaries of defined benefit programs that guaranteed them an income from the day they retired until the day they died. That number is now only 3 percent.

[8] Peter Drucker, *The Unseen Revolution: How Pension Fund Socialism Came to America* (New York: 1976), p. 36: The ESOPS promoted by Louis Kelso and others "would make the workers 'owners' but, for half or more of them, in bankrupt companies or declining industries, thus depriving them of the pension they need."

> As I see it, heightened job insecurity explains a significant part of the restraint on compensation and the consequent muted price inflation.
>
> Surveys of workers have highlighted this extraordinary state of affairs. In 1991, at the bottom of the recession, a survey of workers at large firms indicated that 25 percent feared being laid off. In 1996, despite the sharply lower unemployment rate and the demonstrably tighter labor market ... 46 percent were fearful of a job layoff.[9]

A major reason why U.S. wages were failing to rise despite the increase in labor productivity from fewer strikes and more intensive working conditions (via attrition spreading the work among fewer employees), Chairman Greenspan pointed out to the U.S. Senate, was that workers were afraid to go on strike or even to complain about working conditions for fear of losing their paychecks, defaulting on their mortgage and falling behind on their monthly credit card bills and seeing their interest rates explode as their credit ratings declined. In July 1997 testimony he said that a major factor contributing to the "extraordinary" and "exceptional" U.S. economic performance was "a heightened sense of job insecurity and, as a consequence, subdues wage gains."[10] Bob Woodward described him as calling this the "traumatized worker" effect.

Median U.S. household income rose by a mere 15 percent during 2001-06 while mortgage credit inflated the cost of housing by 74 percent. Heavy mortgage debt and other housing and living costs have made workers feel one paycheck away from homelessness. As employees became debt ridden, widespread home ownership became a euphemism for a cowed labor force.

---

[9] Statement by Alan Greenspan, Chairman, Board of Governors of the Federal Reserve System, before the Committee on Banking, Housing, and Urban Affairs, U.S. Senate, February 26, 1997 - Statements to the Congress. A Transcript also was published in the April 1997 *Federal Reserve Bulletin*.
[10] Testimony of Chairman Alan Greenspan before the Committee on Banking, Housing, and Urban Affairs, U.S. Senate July 22, 1997: "The Federal Reserve's semiannual monetary policy,"
http://www.federalreserve.gov/boarddocs/hh/1997/july/testimony.htm

Austerity's squeeze on labor is even tighter now that rents are rising along with unemployment and shifts to part-time or lower-wage jobs.

Financial appropriation of labor's disposable personal income

The classical idea of a post-industrial leisure economy was to free nations from rent and interest overhead to bring prices in line with necessary direct costs of production, with basic services being subsidized by governments out of progressive taxes and new money creation. Instead, today's financialized vision of free markets limits the range of choice. Families can choose *which* bank to borrow from, *which* home to buy with a 30-year working-life mortgage, and *which* college to take out an education loan to attend. But whatever their choice, they must spend their life working mainly to pay banks for the credit needed to survive in today's world.

Financializing education

Next to home ownership, education is the path to middle class prosperity. It has become so expensive that student loans are now the second largest category of personal debt (over $1 trillion as of 2014, exceeding the volume of credit-card debt). Carrying charges on this debt absorb over 25 percent of the income of many graduates from lower-income families.

Saddling students and new homebuyers with debt has turned their hopes and ambition into a road to insolvency. Something must give way when earnings are unable to cover the stipulated debt service. If banks do not write down their loans, foreclosure time arrives and assets will be forfeited.

The 2005 U.S. bankruptcy code reversed a long trend toward greater protection of debtors. Written largely by bank and credit-card lobbyists, the new law makes it harder to write off personal debts in general, and nearly impossible for student loans to be cleared. The effect is to turn many graduates into indentured servants, obliged to spend much of their working lives paying off the debt taken on to obtain a degree. Many make ends meet by living at home with their parents. Inability to save enough for a home of their own slows the rate of marriages and family formation.

Privatizing and financializing the educational system raises the cost of living imposes an access fee on the entry point into the middle class job market. This reverses the policy long followed by the United States, Germany and other successful nations that made their economies more competitive by providing education and other basic services freely or at subsidized rates. Creating a need for loans at the educational choke point turns universities into vehicles for banks to earn government-guaranteed interest.

Much as interest charges on home mortgages end up giving banks a larger sum than the sales price received by the sellers, student loan payments often give the bank as much interest income over time as the college or trade school has received as tuition. Consumer credit, home mortgage and education loans thus treat the labor force much as feudal landlords treated the land and its occupants: simply as a source of tribute.

From finance capitalism to neofeudalism

Hiding behind an Orwellian rhetoric that inverts the classical idea of a free market, financial planners are leading the world down the path that autocratic Spain and France took five hundred years ago. Without contributing to production, *rentier* income is overwhelmingly responsible for the wealthiest 1% obtaining 73 percent of U.S. income growth since the 2008 crash, while the 99% have seen their net worth decline. Yet the Piketty's much-applauded neoliberal attempt to explain today's economic polarization makes no mention of finance and rent-seeking, so his remedy does not include focusing tax policy on *rentier* income or de-privatizing basic infrastructure monopolies by restoring a mixed public/private economy.[11]

The drive to widen political democracy was expected to avoid this fate by putting in place fiscal and regulatory checks against *rentiers* so that industrial capitalism could use its surplus to expand markets and, in the process, raise living standards. But after World War I changed the course of economic history, Thorstein Veblen explained how Wall Street's financial engineering was undercutting industrial capital. But the idea of asset-price

---

[11] I elaborate this point in "Piketty vs. the classical economic reformers," in Edward Fullbrook and Jamie Morgan, eds., *Piketty's Capital in the Twenty-First Century* (World Economics Association Books, 2014), pp. 189-202.

inflation as a financial strategy extending credit in ways decoupled from helping economies grow was nowhere on the intellectual horizon.

The Great Depression and its debt deflation showed that the antithesis of widespread property ownership in today's world turns out to be finance capitalism, not socialism. Paying bankers and bondholders at the "real" economy's expense is antithetical to that of industrial capitalism. The financial business plan is to turn economies into a set of rent traps, carving out privileges to extract monopoly rent – and for banks to finance the purchase and sale of such rights at interest. Instead of lowering the cost of basic services to make economies more competitive, the effect is to load them down with debt to extract interest, fees and *rentier* overhead. This destructive policy inflates the economy's cost structure by building in higher user fees for the privatized monopolies and a rising flow of debt service to bankers, while imposing debt and rent deflation on the core economy.

Wall Street, the City of London, Frankfurt and other financial centers have replaced government to become our epoch's central planners. Their business plan is to draw into their own hands all the economy's net income, followed by the assets that produce it. So the shift of economic and social planning into the hands of financial managers has undercut the U.S. and British economies as industrial exporters. It is easier to make money by financial manipulation than by the hard work of designing new products, organizing production facilities, hiring and training labor and a marketing and sales force.

Financializing the income streams from these tollbooth privileges is not about earning profits by tangible productive capital investment. It is about appropriating the public domain on credit. This financial mode of expropriation reverses the happy assumption that the momentum of historical progress will, by itself, ensure the primacy of legal systems regulating property and creditor/debtor relationships in the economy's broad long-term interest. The consequence of real estate, corporate control, monopoly rights and access to education and other basic needs being bought increasingly on credit is to turn nominal ownership into mere stewardship on behalf of the banks and bondholders. This locking of populations into paying financial tribute is now portrayed as a moral and legal right.

The *rentier* rake-off of revenue is not a socially necessary cost of production. It makes economies less competitive and post-industrialized. This is not the industrial capitalism envisioned by classical reformers who hoped to free the economy from rent-extracting elites. It is what Hyman Minsky called "money manager capitalism," postindustrial central planning allocating savings and credit to serve the 1% in extractive ways. This neo-*rentier* mode of exploitation is a regression to feudal-type privileges for elites to charge extortionate prices for basic needs. The dynamic pushes a widening swath of the population into austerity and negative equity.

Today's bankers and bondholders are expropriating property owners in ways not anticipated a century ago, when people worried that socialism might play this role. At that time the financial sector appeared to be the strongest buttress of the security of property, if only because collateral needs to be secure in order to be pledged for a loan. But foreclosing creditors always have posed the greatest threat to owner-occupants, asserting their rights to expropriate indebted owners.

The financial fight to reverse classical tax and economic reforms

Instead of governments receiving the rental income of land and natural resources as would occur under classical economics and socialism (at least of the type expressed after Europe's 1848 revolutions), today's financial sector is privatizing these rents for itself. It also attaches itself to industrial capital to obtain its profits as well as the super-profits of monopolies, and to siphon off disposable personal income by obliging homebuyers, students and consumers to pay all their net earnings above subsistence as interest.

This is the essence of debt serfdom. It is how bondholders have hollowed out Greece, Ireland and other debt-torn economies. The way that market equilibrium prices are set for most homebuyers, debt service typically rises to the point where it absorbs the full rental equivalent. Bank mortgages accounted for 60 percent of the overall value of U.S. housing by 2012. As market prices fell while debts remained in place after 2008, the share of homes actually owned by American homeowners had plunged below 40 percent. Families have been pushed, prodded and seduced onto the debt treadmill to pay a rising tribute for what they imagine is to be their economic independence in owning a home. The price is long-term debt servitude, as is getting an education these days.

Much the same predatory dynamic has taken over industry. As Chapter 8 has described, creditors finance corporate raiders who pay out profits as interest and cut back capital investment so as to use earnings simply for stock buybacks to raise its price. Bankers depict their extraction of debt service as a necessary and even natural cost of production, as if the economy would not work without their service of allocating resources to decide who best should receive credit. In reality, banks push debt onto anyone with property to collateralize or earning power to sequester. Their business plan is to maximize financial claims *on* the means of production, up to the limit at which interest absorbs the total disposable income – leaving debtors to perform the economy's actual work.

Pro-creditor ideology depicts loans and credit as enriching borrowers along with lenders in a fair bargain that produces gains for everyone. Borrowers acquiesce in the financialization of real estate as long as they believe that buying homes or companies on credit may enrich them. They are even willing to submit to austerity if they believe it is a necessary interlude to resume economic progress. The reality, of course, is that it sinks them deeper into debt, while widening government budget deficits and leading to demands to cut back social services, starting with pensions and Social Security.

Pro-creditor deceptions require censoring the economic history of how financial dynamics actually have evolved, because the lessons are clear enough over the millennia. Little lending has been productive. Exponentially rising debt service creates a chain reaction that weighs down the economy until it collapses into an inert leaden state.

The destructive character of financial conquest

The financial tragedy of our time is that neither the banking system nor the stock market is funding tangible capital formation to increase production, employment and living standards. Credit is created and lent out to bid up prices of existing real estate, stocks and bonds. Instead of raising equity capital to alleviate debt pressures, the stock market has become a vehicle for corporate raiding and leveraged buyouts on credit, replacing stock with high-interest bonds. At its most vulgarized level of Alan Greenspan, Milton Friedman and his Chicago Pinochetistas, making money from privatization, asset-price inflation (the Bubble Economy) and corporate looting is applauded. Ignoring corrosive financialization effects is what makes *rentier* ideology "value-free" and tolerant.

The owl of wisdom only flies at night. Only after a major collapse do the causes become clear regarding the wrongheaded turns that have been taken. It is easier today to see that instead of financing new capital investment, debt-leveraged buyouts have bled companies to pay bondholders and activist shareholders, while the 1% lent out their savings to indebt the 99%. But until Warren Buffet characterized Wall Street's derivatives as weapons of mass financial destruction, most economists failed to recognize the destructive power of debt creation. Its effect is much like the physicist J. Robert Oppenheimer's 1965 description of the atom bomb's Trinity Explosion, recalling the *Bhagavad Gita*'s words of Vishnu: "I am become death, destroyer of worlds."

The collateral damage from such attacks is as irresponsible as it is devastating. From F. Scott Fitzgerald's *The Great Gatsby* to Tom Wolfe's *Bonfire of the Vanities*, novelists have symbolized the very rich as irresponsible auto drivers killing innocent pedestrians. "They were careless people, Tom and Daisy," wrote Fitzgerald; "they smashed up things and creatures and then retreated back into their money or their vast carelessness or whatever it was that kept them together, and let other people clean up the mess they had made." That is what makes the rich different. They are insensitive to how their actions impact the life of others, thoughtless in proclaiming through the universities they fund and the think tanks they endow that turning over the economy's growth in wealth to the

1% – as has occurred since 2008 – would enable them to help society by helping themselves. Posing as "job creators," *rentiers* claim to be proxies acting like shepherds as a virtual government. Their wealth is supposed to trickle down, somehow. So today's creditors call financialization "wealth creators," whom Goldman Sachs describes as "doing God's work."

The 1% have driven the economy recklessly by the predatory financial policies that enable them to live off the economy, by backing political candidates who dismantle social protection against asset stripping and by endowing business schools and "think tanks" (duly receiving tax credit as if this effort is philanthropic charity) to convince public opinion that there is no such thing as unearned income and wealth.

The effect of this behavior can be seen demographically in statistics of rising suicide rates, shortening life spans and falling birth rates, and with increased suicide rates and emigration. Behind this austerity is the rising burden of debt service. The most notorious examples of neoliberal destructiveness are the post-Soviet states: Russia, the Baltics, and now Ukraine, whose emigrants send remittances back home equal to 5% of their dying nation's GDP.

Despite the fact that nations are legally sovereign, nearly all have agreed to sell off public enterprises to raise foreign exchange to pay the debts they have incurred. The body politic is dismembered, turning public infrastructure into predatory rent-seeking monopolies, increasingly foreign-owned – much as in 17th-century Britain cited above.

Just as the drivers in *Gatsby* and *Bonfire* responsible for crashes left others to bear the blame, so the 1% seeks to shift responsibility onto the financial victims ("the madness of crowds"). Consumers are blamed for not saving more and for needing to break even and live. The population itself is blamed for living longer and creating a "retirement problem" by collecting the Social Security and pensions for which taxpayers must support instead of using FICA paycheck withholding as a ploy to cut progressive tax rates. Governments are blamed for running deficits, despite the fact that they result mainly from tax favoritism to the *rentiers*.

Finance as warfare

The resulting financialization is an economic war – and not all wars end with the victory of the most just and progressive. The end of history is not necessarily utopia. The financial mode of conquest against labor and industry is as devastating today as in the Roman Republic's Social War that marked its transition to Empire in the 1st century BC.

Roman historians blamed their epoch's collapse on creditors reducing the population to debt bondage and outright slavery. It was the dynamics of debt above all that turned the empire into a wasteland. Tacitus reports the words of the Celtic chieftain Calgacus, c. 83 AD, rousing his troops to fight by describing the empire they were to fight against:

> Robbers of the world, having by their universal plunder exhausted the land ... If the enemy is rich, they are rapacious; if he is poor, they lust for dominion; neither the east nor the west has been able to satisfy them. ... To robbery, slaughter, plunder, they give the lying name of empire. They make a wasteland and call it peace.[12]

The peace brought by Rome turned out to be a world whose life reverted to subsistence production on the land as cities became deserted. Rome became the model of what happens to economies that do not annul their debts but polarize between creditors and debtors. Its history – and hence, antiquity – ended in a convulsion of depopulation and a Dark Age.

Commanded by a creditor oligarchy, Rome's imperial conquest was belligerent, with an oppressive anti-labor spirit that Tacitus explained elsewhere (*Agricola* 32): "It belongs to human nature to hate those you have injured." The financial sector's awareness of how rapaciously it obtains its wealth makes it fear and hence hate its victims.

---

[12] *Agricola* 30: *Auferre, trucidare, rapere, falsis nominibus imperium; atque, ubi solitudinem faciunt, pacem appellant.* Translation based on the Loeb Classical Library edition. The chieftain's sentiment can be contrasted to the Orwellian motto "peace given to the world" frequently inscribed on Roman medals, so Tacitus may have been using sarcasm and irony.

So we are brought back to the basic theme of this book: Contrary to expectations when the Industrial Revolution was gaining momentum, predatory finance is stifling industrial potential, raising the specter of lapsing back into the ancient usury dynamic with exponentially accruing debt dependency. Much like creditors in ancient Rome, today's financial power seeks to replace democracy with oligarchy, austerity and neofeudalism. We are seeing a resurgence of "primitive accumulation" by debt creation, foreclosure and privatization.

CHAPTER 2
Piketty vs. the classical economic reformers

Thomas Piketty has done a great service in collating the data of many countries to quantify the ebb and flow of their distribution of wealth and income. For hundreds of pages and tables, his measurements confirm what most people sense without needing statistical proof. Across the globe, the top 1% have increased their share of wealth and income to the steepest extreme since the Gilded Age of the late 19th and early 20th century.

The Federal Reserve's 2013 *Survey of Consumer Finances* shows that economic polarization has accelerated since the 2008 crash. The 0.1% of Americans have pulled even further ahead of the rest of the 1%, who in turn have widened their gains over the remainder of the 10%. At the bottom of the pyramid, the poorest 10% have faired even worse than the next lowest. The economy is operating like a centrifuge separating rich from poor. But neither Piketty nor the Fed makes an attempt to explain the dynamics causing this polarization. They merely measure its broad parameters.

Some reviewers have labeled Piketty's statistics and policy proposals as Marxist, partly because the title of his book – *Capital in the Twenty-First Century* – suggests that it might aim at updating of Marx's *Capital*.[1] Even Martin Wolf writes of Piketty's book that, "in its scale and sweep it brings us back to the founders of political economy."[2] But apart from seeing inequality as a social threat, there is little similarity either in Piketty's analysis or in his proposed policy remedies.

---

[1] See for instance Steven Erlanger, "Taking on Adam Smith (and Karl Marx)," *The New York Times*, April 20, 2014.
[2] Martin Wolf, "Inequality time," *Financial Times*, April 19, 2014.

Marx followed in the classical tradition of Francois Quesnay, Adam Smith, David Ricardo and John Stuart Mill in defining economic rent (including natural resource rent and monopoly rent from legal privileges or control of access point to key infrastructure monopolies) as the excess of price over intrinsic labor-cost value. Volumes II and III of Marx's *Capital* extend value theory to the exploitation of industrial wage labor by capitalists. Using the labor theory of value to define extractive rentier or capitalist exploitation is what distinguishes classical political economy from the post-classical reaction against Marx and other reformers and critics gaining political influence by the turn of the 20th century.

The statistical sources used by Piketty reflect this reaction against treating *rentier* income as unearned. Post-classical theory insists that all income is earned productively, with no source of gain less productive than any other. Making money by privatizing public monopolies and cutting services, or simply price gouging to cover higher costs of interest and dividends, management fees, higher executive salaries and stock options is treated as economically productive as building new factories and hiring employees.

Limiting Picketty's reform proposals to what anti-reform statistics reveal

Piketty sought to explain the ebb and flow of polarization by suggesting a basic mathematical law: when wealth is unequally distributed and returns to capital (interest, dividends and capital gains) exceed the rise in overall income (as measured by GDP), economies polarize in favor of capital owners. Unlike the classical economists, he does not focus on *rentier* gains by real estate owners, their bankers, corporate raiders and financiers, privatizers and other rent seekers.

Piketty is limited by the available statistical sources, because any accounting format reflects the economic theory that defines its categories. Neither the National Income and Product Accounts (NIPA) nor the Internal Revenue Service's *Statistics on Income* in the United States define the specific form that the wealth buildup takes. Most textbook models focus on tangible investment in means of production (plant and equipment, research and development). But industrial profits on such investment have fallen relative to more passive gains from asset-price inflation (rising debt-fueled prices for real estate, stocks and bonds), financial speculation (arbitrage, derivatives trading and credit default insurance), and land rent, natural resource rent (oil and gas, minerals), monopoly rent (including patent rights), and legal privileges topped by the ability of banks to create interest-bearing credit.

A byproduct of this value-free view of wealth is that Piketty suggests an equally value-free remedy for inequality: a global estate tax with a progressive wealth and income tax. Not only is this almost impossible to enforce politically, but a general tax on wealth or income does not discriminate between what is earned "productively" and what is squeezed out by rent extraction or obtained by capital gains.

The advantage of classical economic theory's focus on rent extraction, financialization and debt-leveraged asset-price ("capital") gains is that each form of "unearned" wealth and income has a different set of remedies. But to Picketty's sources – and hence to his analysis – wealth is wealth, income is income, and that is that. He is obliged to make his solution as general as his statistics that define the problem.

Taxing all forms of income or wealth at the same rate does not favor industrial investment over financial engineering. It does not reverse today's fiscal subsidy treating interest as tax-deductible. This tax preference for buying companies on credit – using their earnings to pay interest to bondholders and bankers – enables the 1% to obtain a much higher payout in the form of interest than by dividends on equity financing. The tax collector loses in favor of creditors – and taxes consumers and wage earners to make up the shortfall. Meanwhile, low taxes on capital gains encourage corporate managers to use earnings for stock buybacks to bid up their prices. Piketty's book does not address these tax preferences and distortions favoring the 1%.

Why is inequality increasing? False leads that Piketty avoids, but does not controvert

Piketty shows that inequality is rising, but his broad formula relating overall financial returns (r) to the overall rate of economic growth (g) does not explain how policies have driven the turnaround since 1980. But at least his broad treatment of *rentiers* does not succumb to apologetics based on age and educational levels.

The "life cycle" theory of savings depicts individuals borrowing to consume more when young, and repay out of incomes expected to rise during their working life. They pay interest to "patient" savers who defer their own consumption in order to earn interest. This "abstinence" theory blames debtors for their plight of needing credit to get by in today's world. Inherited wealth seems to play no role, as if everyone starts from the same economic point. Also absent from this "pay later" view is the fact that real wages have stopped rising since 1980. Upward mobility is much more difficult to achieve, and most debtors have to pay by working even harder for lower wages.

It is not by deferring consumption that inheritors obtain their wealth. As Marx put it, it is absurd to view the Rothschilds as growing so rich simply by being Europe's most "abstinent" consumers. And on the macroeconomic level, this individualistic "life-cycle theory" of interest ignores the fact that the economy is an overall system whose volume of debt grows exponentially from one generation to the next as savings accrue and are augmented by new electronic bank credit – extracting interest from debtors.

Another diversionary explanation of wealth disparity is educational status, duly dubbed "human capital" on the logic that each academic step adds to the stream of future earnings. The idea is that better-educated individuals at the best schools earn more – justifying student debt. One CEO of a Fortune 500 company has assured me that the reason he is so rich is because he is so smart and well educated. Other corporate executives tell me that the reason they hire economics PhDs is that it shows that the prospective employee is willing to work hard for a goal to get a better job. The tacit message is that such PhDs have learned to accept writing economic fictions to get ahead. But all you really need is greed, and that can't be taught in school.

On the negative side of the relationship between education and net worth, schooling has become so expensive and debt leveraged that the burden of student loans is keeping recent graduates living at home with their parents instead of being able to start families in homes of their own. For-profit technical schools such as the University of Phoenix have notoriously low graduation rates, but use government-guaranteed loans to create an artificial market selling dreams that end in jobless student-loan peonage taking its place alongside debt serfdom for homebuyers paying mortgages.

Matters are even worse than Piketty's measure of inequality shows. He refers to gross income, not the net earnings *after* meeting basic expenses. To make wages conceptually symmetrical with profits or rents – corporate profits or cash flow *after* meeting the costs of production – the appropriate measure would be wages after meeting basic living expenses. That is why net worth measures are more important than income.

What U.S. official statistics call "disposable income" – paychecks *after* taxes and FICA withholding – is not all that disposable. Recipients must pay their monthly "nut": debt service on bank loans and credit cards, home mortgages or rent, pension fund and health insurance contributions, and other basic expenses needed simply to break even, such as food and transportation to and from work. Faced with these monthly obligations, a rising proportion of the labor force finds itself with scant savings. Hence the "traumatized worker" effect, "one paycheck away from homelessness," too fearful to strike or even to complain about working conditions or the lack of wage increases.

The upshot is that most wealth takes the form of what classical economists characterized as unearned income, mainly from the FIRE (finance, insurance and real estate) sector: interest and various forms of economic rent, inherited wealth and "capital" gains, not to speak of tax avoidance, stock options and other favoritism for *rentiers*.

Piketty's statistics show a number of turning points in the share of wages compared to returns to capital (interest, dividends and capital gains). The Gilded Age was followed by a move toward greater equality during 1914–50. A progressive U.S. income tax was legislated in 1913, taxing capital gains as normal income – at a high rate. (Only about 1 percent of Americans initially had to file tax returns.) The Great War was followed by the financial crash of 1929, the Great Depression and World War II that destroyed capital or taxed it more heavily. A period of relative stability followed in the 1960s and 70s as progressive taxes and public regulation were maintained.

The 1980 turning point in wealth and income distribution

The great turning point occurred in 1980 after the victory of Margaret Thatcher's Conservatives in Britain and Ronald Reagan in the United States. Progressive taxes were rolled back, public enterprises were privatized and debts soared – owed mainly to the wealthy. Interest rates have been driven down to historic lows – and after the crash of 2008 the aim of Quantitative Easing has been to re-inflate asset prices by reviving a Bubble Economy aiming mainly at "capital" gains for wealth-holders. These trends have led wealth to soar and become concentrated in the hands of the top 1% and other wealthy families, first during the post-1980 bubble and even more during its post-2008 collapse.

1. Interest rates and easier credit terms promoting debt leveraging (pyramiding)

Interest rates determine the rate at which a given flow of income, interest or dividends is capitalized into mortgage loans, bond or stock prices. Rising steadily from 1951, loans by U.S. banks to prime corporate customers reached a peak of 20 percent by yearend 1979. At that rate it was nearly impossible to make a profit or capital gain by borrowing to buy housing, commercial real estate, stocks or bonds.

Then, for more than thirty years, interest rates plunged to all-time lows. This decline led bankers and bondholders to lend more and more against income-yielding properties. As mortgage interest rates fell, larger bank loans could be afforded out of existing income and rent, because a property is worth whatever a bank will lend against it. This "creates wealth" by purely financial means – an explosion of bank credit financing capital gains over and above current income. Prices for bonds enjoyed the greatest bull market in history.

In addition to lowering interest rates, banks stretched out the maturities and also required lower down payments to attract more customers hoping to get rich by going deeper into debt. And until 2008, real estate – the economy's largest asset – rose almost steadily. But a byproduct of debt leveraging is that mortgage holders receive a rising proportion of the rental income of property. Home ownership was becoming a road to debt peonage, as owners' equity declined as a share of the property's price.

Much the same phenomenon was occurring in industry after 1980. Innovations in leveraged buyouts enabled corporate raiders, management teams and ambitious financial empire-builders to buy companies on credit, paying earnings to bondholders instead of reinvesting in the business (or paying income taxes). Capital gains were achieved by bidding up stock prices by share buybacks and higher dividend payouts, while cutting costs by downsizing and scaling back pension plans.

Most money is not being made by tangible capital investment but financially. Stock buybacks are being financed even with borrowed funds – going into debt to create short-term capital gains for managers whose pay is tied to stock options. "In 2012, the 500 highest paid US executives made on average $30.3 [million] each … More than 80 per cent of it came in the form of stock options or stock awards. Their incentives are skewed towards extracting value from the companies they run, rather than creating future value."[3]

Gains by the 1% of this sort are not an inherently natural law. "Greed will always be with us. Dumb laws are optional," the *Financial Times* writer just quoted observes. This perception is missing in Piketty's analysis. Thinking about inequality simply in terms of comparing the return to capital to overall economic growth leaves little room for public policy. And in the absence of government taking the lead, planning shifts to Wall Street and other financial centers. The result is as centrally planned an economy as Hayek warned against in *The Road to Serfdom*. But it is planned financially, for purely pecuniary gain, not for economic growth or industrial capital formation as such.

---

[3] Edward Luce, "The short-sighted US buyback boom," *Financial Times*, September 22, 2014.

This means that in order to preserve its momentum, financialization evolves into Bubble Economies, requiring ever larger injections of credit to bid up asset prices by enough to cover the interest charges falling due. Wealth-holders can gain only as long as asset prices grow as exponentially as the compounding of interest. This requires that banks continue to lend, or that governments bail out financial markets, *e.g.* by the Federal Reserve's Quantitative Easing or Mario Draghi's "Whatever it takes" at the European Central Bank.

Bankers promote fiscal policies to encourage debt leveraging by focusing the public's attention on personal gains to be made by borrowing to buy assets expected to rise in price. What is suppressed is recognition that the wealthiest layer of the economy gets most of the gains while homebuyers, industry and governments go deeper into debt.

2.   *Privatization and rent seeking*

The second major trend concentrating wealth in the hands of the ultra-rich since 1980 has been privatization. Led ideologically by Margaret Thatcher in Britain after 1979 (applauding Chile's "free market" privatization at gunpoint under General Pinochet after 1973), the pretense is that private management is inherently more efficient than public enterprise. Yet in contrast to the public interest in lowering prices – by subsidizing basic services to make economies more competitive – the aim of private owners is to install tollbooths to extract economic rent.

Under the neoliberal Pinochet-Thatcher style privatizations, capital investments in transportation, power, communications and other basic commanding heights were sold off, mainly on credit. This was the opposite of reform policy a century ago socializing pensions and health care, water, roads and other essential services. Key infrastructure was to be kept in the public domain or (in the case of heavy industry such as British steel) nationalized. But since 1980 infrastructure has been privatized into "tollbooth" opportunities to extract financial returns (interest and capital gains) and monopoly rent.

The richest individuals in the former Soviet Union and many Third World countries have gained their wealth by insider dealings to obtain such *rentier* privileges. In Mexico, Carlos Slim's fortune comes from charging high telephone rates increasing the cost of living and of doing business. This is how America's railroad barons became the Gilded Age elite, the last time that wealth inequality was as high as it is today. The U.S. stock market was largely a market in shares for railroads, much as stock markets in other countries dealt mainly in canals and commercial monopolies or trusts.

This concentration of wealth was achieved by rent extraction, bribery and fraud, facilitated by ideological patter that claims any way of transferring property into private ownership would help society grow richer faster. Piketty's point is simply that having been appropriated, such wealth takes a financial form, which should be taxed to rectify matters. He sees no need to reverse privatization, to change today's tax favoritism for *rentiers*, regulate monopoly prices, enact an excess-profit tax or minimum wage laws, full employment policies, debt writedowns and other specific remedies.

3. The tax shift off wealth and capital gains onto wages and consumer spending

An array of tax shifts has favored the wealthy. In addition to rolling back progressive income tax rates, the "small print" gives special exemptions for the FIRE sector (finance, insurance and real estate). Corporate industry and the wealthy are emulating the oil industry's pioneering tactics to declare their profits in offshore tax-avoidance centers. Real estate investors can pretend that their buildings are depreciating so fast that this fictitious book-loss offsets their otherwise declarable rental income. (Homeowners are not allowed to make such a deduction; only absentee owners can do so.)

Permitting interest payments to be tax-deductible subsidizes debt leveraging at the tax collector's expense. Capital gains are not taxed if they are invested to buy yet more property, or bequeathed when the owner dies. The effect is that in addition to receiving the lion's share of tax cuts, the 1% to 10% receive most of the interest and asset-price gains bid up on bank credit.

Governments are obliged to make up the fiscal shortfall resulting from favoring the wealthy by raising sales taxes on consumers and wage earners, *e.g.*, by Europe's value-added tax (VAT). U.S. state and local governments have replaced the property tax (which provided three-quarters of their fiscal revenue a century ago, but now accounts for only one-sixth) with local sales and income taxes that fall mainly on consumers.

Un-taxing *rentier* wealth favors the 1% who hold the 99% increasingly in debt. To make matters worse, taxing labor and industry instead of *rentiers* increases the cost of living and doing business, shrinking the economy and hence employment and wage rates.

4. *Financing budget deficits via bondholders instead of government money creation*

World War I (like America's Civil War) showed that governments could finance their own spending by "greenbacks" instead of borrowing from bondholders. But the latter wanted to keep government debt financing for themselves – and to keep governments on a short monetary leash as a means of controlling their policies.

At issue is whether economies will depend on credit creation by and for the 1%, or whether governments will self-finance deficits to promote full employment. Opponents of central bank money creation accuse central bank financing of being inherently inflationary, leading almost inexorably to Weimar-era style hyperinflation. The claim is that private bankers provide more responsible funding. But in practice the 1% promote policies that augment their own wealth by inflating asset prices on credit owed mainly to themselves.

Meanwhile, blocking government self-financing is *de*flationary. By running a budget surplus in the late 1990s, the Clinton administration obliged the U.S. economy to rely on commercial banks for its increased money supply. The result was a sharp rise in the debt overhead (at rising interest rates). Likewise in today's Eurozone, the European Central Bank's refusal to finance government deficits – and limiting budget deficits to only 3% of GDP – is turning the continent into a dead zone.

In contrast to public spending to promote growth and employment for the economy at large, bank credit "creates wealth" mainly by lending against property and financial securities and thus inflating asset prices, not by funding new tangible capital investment. This underlying contrast is a major factor explaining why the 1% advocates policies that increase the market valuation of its wealth vis-à-vis labor's wages. Any reform policy to reverse today's economic polarization needs to address this monetary and fiscal contrast.

5. Debt deflation

The main long-term dynamic holding back recovery in Europe and North America is the debt overhead – a flow of interest upward to bank bondholders and other creditors and "savers." The economy has become a debt pyramid diverting rent and profits as well as wages to pay debt service. Like corporate profits, a rising bite out of wages is being paid out as debt service, especially as wages have merely moved sideways since the late 1970s. Wages hitherto spent on consumer goods are paid to creditors, shrinking markets in the "real" non-*rentier* economy.

Despite his criticism of the financial sector, Piketty does not address the debt, credit or monetary dimensions of economic polarization. He proposes simply to tax the financialized economy that this debt pyramid has created, leaving in place the debt corner into which the 1% have painted the economy. It is difficult to see how a progressive income and estate tax alone can reverse the trend toward polarization without writing down today's debt overhead.

A major reason why the 1% have increased their gains since 2008 is that the Treasury and Federal Reserve bailed out banks, their bondholders and uninsured large depositors instead of obliging them to absorb the loss from having lent much more than borrowers were able to pay. These bailouts, and the Federal Reserve's subsequent Quantitative Easing to re-inflate real estate and other asset prices, were the only occasions on which banks have applauded government money creation – when it is to pay *them*, not to spur tangible investment and employment in the non-*rentier* economy.

33

These government policies are not the result of an inherent mathematical law about the return to capital vis-à-vis that of the non-*rentier* economy – GDP and wages. Reversing the widening inequality between finance capital and wage labor entails going far beyond Piketty's advocacy of more progressive income and wealth taxation. While certainly desirable, these taxes by themselves would leave in place the political, financial and privatized rent-extracting structures that serve the 1% to support their debt claims and tollbooth charges on the economy at large.

Piketty's narrow solution reflects the limited scope of his analysis. The 2008 crisis offered an opportunity much like wartime and the Great Depression to wipe out the financial buildup. But the response was to prevent financial losses by bankers and bondholders. Instead of governments acting to restore prosperity, they imposed austerity to squeeze out enough revenue to save banks from insolvency.

Piketty does not call for reversing the debt leveraging that has inflated asset prices, much less writing down the debts that hold the 99% in financial bondage. He accepts the status quo but would tax inherited wealth and restore an 80 percent tax rate such as typified the 1940s and '50s on incomes above $500,000 or $1 million, as if the wealthy will not circumvent such policies by the stratagems put in place in recent decades.

Ideological support for the 1%'s conquest of the 99%

Despite Piketty's focus on today's financial *rentiers* instead of landlords as the major idle rich class, he does not see that sustaining its dominance over the rest of the economy involves the political sphere. He accepts the political and legal environment for granted. His limited vision is what attracts a New York fund manager writing in the *Wall Street Journal*: "Thomas Piketty likes capitalism because it efficiently allocates resources. But he does not like how it allocates income."[4] As if the two can be separated!

The economy is polarizing because of how the 1% use their wealth. If they invested their fortunes productively as "job creators" – as mainstream

---

[4] Daniel Shuchman, "Thomas Piketty Revives Marx for the 21st Century," *Wall Street Journal*, April 22, 2014.

textbooks describe them as doing – there would be some logic in today's tax favoritism and financial bailouts. *Rentier* elites would be doing what governments are supposed to do. Instead, today's financial oligarchy lends out its savings to indebt the economy at large, and uses its gains to buy control of government to extract more special privileges, tax favoritism and rent-extraction opportunities by political campaign financing in the United States (unlimited since the Supreme Court's Citizens United ruling) and by lobbying.

Politics and the legal system have become part of the market in the sense of being up for sale. As in consumer advertising, ideological engineering is used to "manufacture consent," using the mass media to broadcast an anti-tax and anti-regulatory ethic. Thorstein Veblen described the tactic a century ago in *Higher Learning in America* (1904). Business schools have been endowed, economic prizes awarded and public relations "think tanks" staffed with credentialed spokesmen to shape popular perceptions to accept widening financial inequality as natural and even desirable.

Piketty's statistics show that inequality of wealth and income distribution is higher in the United States than in Europe, but he does not explain that this is largely because public spending and subsidies to promote employment and living conditions are much stronger outside of the United States. His proposed tax remedy does not include structural reforms, much less a public option for banking and de-privatization of the infrastructure still being sold to rent-extractors on credit.

Focusing mainly on the exponential accrual of inherited wealth, Piketty rightly warns of a lapse of economic democracy back into "patrimonial capitalism," a *rentier* economy controlled by hereditary dynasties. The world is seeing a retrogression of economic democracy back into *rentier* oligarchy. This prospect makes it all the more important to understand the dynamics that are endowing such dynasties. But Piketty's formula about the rate of return on capital (r) exceeding the rate of economic growth (g) does not explain how this political maneuvering over public policy affects this ratio. His statistics on inequality in themselves say nothing about the tactics of class warfare to prevent the minimum wage from being raised in the United States, or to impose austerity rather than full employment policies.

As Adam Smith pointed out, the rate of profit is often highest in countries going fastest to ruin. If there are internal contradictions, what may bring the rate of return (Piketty's r, increasingly based on debt service and asset-price inflation) back in line with the ability to pay out of growth (Piketty's g)? Would his proposed global tax on wealth and high incomes be sufficient to reverse today's widening inequality without changing the fiscal and social-economic structures that the financial oligarchy has created to prevent such a reversal?

It was by dealing with these structures to free industrial capitalism from the vestiges of feudalism that the classical economists were revolutionary, above all by taxing absentee-owned land. So radical was this drive to subordinate the growth of *rentier* wealth to serve society at large that despite almost winning by the early 20th century, it faltered. Marx extended this post-feudal revolution to the industrial economy in a way that reflected the interest of the working majority. But progress along these lines is now in danger of being rolled back under pressure of financial austerity.

When it comes to proposing an alternative, Piketty is no such radical. His version of a singular tax solution – a heavy estate tax and a global tax on the higher wealth and income brackets – does not follow the classical reformers' key distinction between *rentier* "free lunch" income and wealth earned productively. It does not counter the financialization of industry, reverse privatization carve-outs from the public domain, or see a need for a public option to finance budget deficits and retail banking. In that respect his remedy is in line with the post-classical "value-free" reaction denying that any forms of income are unearned and outright predatory.

Piketty's book provides a comprehensive description of the symptoms of pro-*rentier* policy as measured by the inequality of overall wealth and income distribution. But without analyzing or diagnosing the array of strategies by which *rentier* wealth has rolled back earlier policies toward greater economic equality of after-tax income and wealth, it cannot prescribe a remedy to stop today's economic polarization at its taproot.

CHAPTER 3

Incorporating the *rentier* sectors into a financial model[1]

Michael Hudson and Dirk Bezemer

Abstract

Current macroeconomics ignores the roles that rent, debt and the financial sector play in shaping our economy. We discuss the Classical view on rents and policy responses to the *rentier* sector in the 19th century. The finance, insurance & real estate sector is today's incarnation of the *rentier* sector. This paper shows how financial flows can be conceptually and statistically studied separately from (but interacting with) the real sector. We discuss finance's interaction with government and with the international economy.

[Key words: asset prices, debt, deflation, FIRE-sector, *rentier* sectors]

1. Introduction

Now that the Bubble Economy has given way to debt deflation, the world is discovering the shortcoming of models that fail to explain how most credit creation today 1) inflates asset prices without raising commodity prices or wage levels, and 2) creates a reciprocal flow of debt service. This debt service tends to rise as a proportion of personal and business income, outgrowing the ability of debtors to pay — leading to 3) debt deflation. The only way to prevent this

---

[1] An earlier version of this chapter can be found in Hudson's book, *The Bubble and Beyond*. The authors declare no conflict of interest.

phenomenon from plunging economies into depression and keeping them there is 4) to write down the debts so as to free revenue for spending once again on goods and services.

By promoting a misleading view of how the economy works, the above omissions lead to a policy that fails to prevent debt bubbles or deal effectively with the ensuing depression. To avoid a replay of the recent financial crisis – and indeed, to extricate economies from their present debt strait-jacket that subordinates recovery to the overhang of creditor claims (that is, saving the banks from taking a loss on their bad loans and gambles) – it is necessary to explain how credit creation inflates housing and other asset prices, while interest and other financial charges deflate the 'real' economy, holding down commodity prices, shrinking markets and employment, and holding down wages in a downward economic spiral. We are dealing with two price trends that go in opposite directions: asset prices and commodity prices. It therefore is necessary to explain how credit expansion pushes asset prices up while simultaneously causing debt deflation.

Yet the typical MV=PT monetary and price model focused on commodity prices and wages, not on the asset prices inflated by debt leveraging. Similarly, today's Dynamic Stochastic General Equilibrium (or DSGE) models are characterized by the "absence of an appropriate way of modeling financial markets" (Tovar 2008, p. 29). While Schumpeter (1934, p. 95) already noted that "processes in terms of means of payment are not merely reflexes of processes in terms of goods. In every possible strain, with rare unanimity, even with impatience and moral and intellectual indignation, a very long line of theorists have assured us of the opposite" this finds no place in DSGE models or, for that matter macroeconomics in the last decades. Cecchetti et al (2011, p. 2) describe current practice in writing that "for a macroeconomist working to construct a theoretical structure for understanding the economy as a whole, debt is... trivial... because (in a closed economy) it is net zero – the liabilities of all borrowers always exactly match the assets of all lenders. ...With no active role for money, integrating credit in the mainstream framework has proven to be difficult". And yet credit and its counterpart, debt, have shaped our economic systems since prehistory (Hudson 2004). Understanding how credit is used is therefore a sine qua non for understanding our economy. That requires, in turn, to think about a fundamentally different model which can replace DGSE type models as the standard for analysis. Only then can the "naked emperor be dethroned" (Keen 2011).

2. Finance is not *the* economy

In the real world most credit today is spent to buy assets already in place, not to create new productive capacity. Some 80 percent of bank loans in the English-speaking world are real estate mortgages, and much of the balance is lent against stocks and bonds already issued. Banks lend to buyers of real estate, corporate raiders, ambitious financial empire-builders, and to management for debt-leveraged buyouts. A first approximation of this trend is to chart the share of bank lending that goes to the 'Fire, Insurance and Real Estate' sector, aka the nonbank financial sector. Graph 1 shows that its ratio to GDP has quadrupled since the 1950s. The contrast is with lending to the real sector, which has remained about constant relative to GDP. This is how our debt burden has grown.

Graph 1: Private debt growth is due to lending to the FIRE sector: the US, 1952-2007

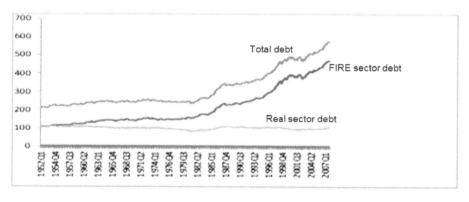

Source: Bezemer (2012) based on US flow of fund data, BEA 'Z' tables

What is true for America is true for many other countries: mortgage lending and other household debt have been "the final stage in an artificially extended Ponzi Bubble" as Keen (2009, pp. 347–357) shows for Australia. Extending credit to purchase assets already in place bids up their price. Prospective homebuyers need to take on larger mortgages to obtain a home. The effect is to turn property rents into a flow of mortgage interest. These payments divert the revenue of consumers and businesses from being spent on consumption or new capital investment. The effect is *de*flationary for the economy's product markets, and hence consumer prices and employment, and therefore wages. This is why we had a long period of low cpi inflation but skyrocketing asset price inflation. The two trends are linked.

Debt-leveraged buyouts and commercial real estate purchases turn business cash flow (ebitda: earnings before interest, taxes, depreciation and amortization) into interest payments. Likewise, bank or bondholder financing of public debt (especially in the Eurozone, which lacks a central bank to monetize such debt) has turned a rising share of tax revenue into interest payments. As creditors recycle their receipts of interest and amortization (and capital gains) into new lending to buyers of real estate, stocks and bonds, a rising share of employee income, real estate rent, business revenue and even government tax revenue is diverted to pay debt service. By leaving less to spend on goods and services, the effect is to reduce new investment and employment. Contemporary evidence for major OECD economies since the 1980s shows that rising capital gains may indeed divert finance away from the real sector's productivity growth (Stockhammer 2004, pp. 719-41) and more generally that 'financialization' (Epstein 2005) has hurt growth and incomes. Money created for capital gains has a small propensity to be spent by their *rentier* owners on goods and services, so that an increasing proportion of the economy's money flows are diverted to circulation in the financial sector. So wages do not increase, even as prices for property and financial securities rise – just the well-known trend that we have seen in the Western world since the 1970s, and which persists into the post- 2001 Bubble Economy.

It is especially the case since 1991 in the post-Soviet economies, where neoliberal (that is, pro- financial) policy makers have had a free hand to shape tax and financial policy in favor of banks (mainly foreign bank branches). Latvia is cited as a neoliberal success story, but it would be hard to find an example where *rentier* income and prices have diverged more sharply from wages and the 'real' production economy.

The more credit creation takes the form of inflating asset prices – rather than financing purchases of goods and services or direct investment employing labor – the more *de*flationary its effects are on the 'real' economy of production and consumption. Housing and other asset prices crash, causing negative equity. Yet homeowners and businesses still have to pay off their debts. The national income accounts classify this pay- down as 'saving', although the revenue is not available to the debtors doing the 'saving' by 'deleveraging'.

The moral is that using homes as what Alan Greenspan referred to as 'piggy banks' to take out home-equity loans was not really like drawing down a bank account at all. When a bank account is drawn down there is less money available, but no residual obligation to pay. New income can be spent at the discretion of its recipient. But borrowing against a home implies an obligation to set aside future income to pay the banker – and hence a loss of future discretionary spending.

3. Towards a model of financialized economies

Creating a more realistic model of today's financialized economies to trace this phenomenon requires a breakdown of the national income and product accounts (NIPA) to see the economy as a set of distinct sectors interacting with each other. These accounts juxtapose the private and public sectors as far as current spending, saving and taxation is concerned. But the implication is that government budget deficits inflate the private-sector economy as a whole. However, a budget deficit that takes the form of transfer payments to banks, as in the case of the post-September 2008 bank bailout, the Federal Reserve's $2 trillion in cash-for- trash financial swaps and the $700 billion QE2 credit creation by the Federal Reserve to lend to banks at 0.25% interest in

2011, has a different effect from deficits that reflect social spending programs, Social Security and Medicare, public infrastructure investment or the purchase of other goods and services. The effect of transfer payments to the financial sector – as well as the $5.3 trillion increase in US Treasury debt from taking Fannie Mae and Freddie Mac onto the public balance sheet – is to support asset prices (above all those of the banking system), not inflate commodity prices and wages. Similarly, the 2009 'quantitative easing' policy in Britain confused loans used in the real economy (which were stagnating or falling throughout the experiment) with boosting bank balances with the Bank of England which quadrupled over 2009 (Graph 2). Bezemer and Gardiner (2010) show that neither bank loans nor spending nor GDP increased noticeably during or after the exercise, but there was a curious stock market rally during 2009. A London Stock Exchange press release on 29 December 2009 reported that "a record £82.5 billion was raised through new and further issues of equity on the London Stock Exchange during the course of 2009... despite difficult market conditions". Finance is not the economy.

Graph 2: 'Quantitative Easing' in Britain increased bank reserves (right hand axis), but not lending to the real sector (left-hand axis) (billion Pound Sterling)

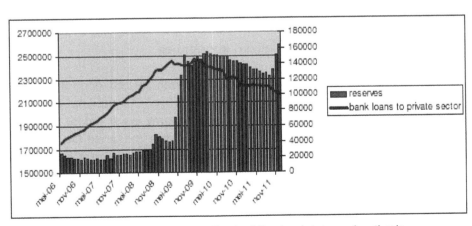

Source: Bezemer (2012) based on Bank of England data and author's calculations

Most models treat the international sector either as a 'leakage' (as Keynes termed foreign trade and capital flows) or as a balancing item in the private/public sector surplus or shortfall (as in the Levy Institute model – see Zezza 2009, pp. 289-310 for an analytical description). But the international sector involves not only export and import trade and other current account items (emigrants' remittances, and above all, military spending) but also foreign investment and income – and foreign central bank reserves held in US Treasury and other securities, that is, loans to the US Government. Capital flows have swollen enormously since the turn of the millennium, and they have increasingly been matched by outflows of investments into dollar-denominated assets held both by private citizens and their governments. This was facilitated by new investment vehicles such as Sovereign Wealth Funds (SWFs). UNCTAD (2011, p. 119) reports 25 newly established SWFs since 2000 only. Thanks to capital inflows, the capital account is now moving independently from the current account. It is not as if the buildup of international savings requires current account surpluses. Even developing countries with current account *deficits* had accumulated foreign reserves as well as private investments in enormous quantities at the eve of the crisis, as Obstfeld (2009) reports. At the heart of this is the US economy and its financial markets. For instance, US consumers and businesses ran a trade deficit, and banks used the entire $700 billion QE2 supply of Fed credit for foreign currency arbitrage and other international speculation, not for lending to the domestic US economy. But the US Treasury received an inflow from foreign central banks building up their dollar reserves by buying Treasury securities and other US financial securities.

Figure 1: Private sector, government sector, international sector

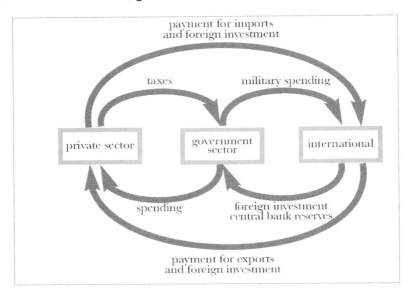

Fig. 1a: US transactions with China, private and government sectors

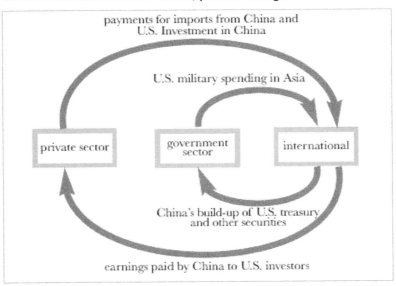

This model can be used to trace US transactions with China. The

economy runs a trade deficit with China, and also a private-sector investment outflow to China. There is some return of earnings from these investments to US companies. But on balance, there is a dollar outflow to China – which also receives dollars from its exports to third countries. China's central bank has recycled most of these dollar receipts to the US Treasury (and earlier, into Fannie Mae bonds and kindred investments), but was not permitted to buy US companies such as Unocal's refinery operations.

This public/private/international model may be made more realistic by treating the financial, insurance and real estate (FIRE) sector as distinct from the underlying production and consumption economy, as motivated in Graph 1.

4. The FIRE sector, rents, and the progressive response

The FIRE sector deals with the economy's balance sheet of assets and debts, real estate, stocks and bonds, mortgages and other bank loans – and the payment of interest, money management commissions and other fees to the financial sector, as well as insurance payments and also rental payments for housing. The FIRE sector is today's form that the *rentier* class takes. *Rentiers* are those who benefit from control over assets that the economy needs to function, and who, therefore, grow disproportionately rich as the economy develops. These proceeds are rents – revenues from ownership "without working, risking, or economizing", as John Stuart Mill (1848) wrote of the landlords of his day, explaining that "they grow richer, as it were in their sleep". Classical economics from Adam Smith onwards analysed rents, its effects, and policies towards rents, but the very concept is lost on today's economics.

Just as landlords were the archetypal *rentiers* of their agricultural societies, so investors, financiers and bankers are in the largest *rentier* sector of today's financialized economies: finance controls the economy's engine of growth, which is credit in all its forms. Economies obviously need banking services, insurance services, and real estate development and so, of course, not all of finance is "without working, risking, or economizing". The problem today remains what it was in the 13th century: how to isolate what is socially necessary for 'retail' banking – processing payments by checks and credit cards, deciding how to relend savings and new credit under normal (non-speculative) conditions – from extortionate charges such as 29% interest on credit cards, penalty fees and other charges in excess of what is socially necessary cost- value.

In principle, all monopolies should be included in this *rentier* sector, as they represent a special privilege (control over markets, especially for necessities) whose return in the form of prices and income in excess of necessary costs of production is a form of economic rent, that is, a transfer payment rather than 'earned' income. But statistically there is no practical way to isolate monopoly rent in the NIPA, as this would include a large part of the information technology sector, pharmaceuticals, and much 'industry'. The ideal conceptual framework for statistics would be to separate economic rent from underlying cost value.

Classical political economists from the Physiocrats through Adam Smith, John Stuart Mill and their Progressive Era followers were reformers in the sense that they treated the *rentier* sectors as extracting transfer payments rather than earning a return for producing actual output ('services'). Their labor theory of value found its counterpart in the 'economic rent theory of prices' to distinguish the necessary costs of production and doing business (reduced ultimately to the value of labor) from 'unearned income' consisting mainly of land rent, monopoly rent, and financial interest and fees. The various categories of *rentier* income were depicted as the 'hollow' element of prices. Land rent, natural resource rent, monopoly rent and returns to privilege (including financial interest and fees) had no counterpart in necessary costs of production. They were historical and institutional products of privileges handed down largely from the medieval conquests that created Europe's landed aristocracy and banking practice that developed largely by insider dealing, legitimized by lending to kings to finance war debts in an epoch when money and credit were the sinews of war. So banking as well as military rivalries for land essentially involved the foreign sector. Mill (1848) asked "What claim have they, on the general principle of social justice, to this accession of riches? In what would they have been wronged if society had, from the beginning, reserved the right of taxing the spontaneous increase of rent, to the highest amount required by financial exigencies?".

The political aim of classical analysis, then, was to minimize the economy's cost structure by freeing industrial capitalism from these carry-overs from feudalism. The reformers' guiding idea was to minimize the role of *rentier* income (economic rent) by public investment, tax policy and regulation. We consider these in turn.

a) Direct public investment in basic infrastructure, including education, transportation systems, communication systems and other enterprises that were long kept in the public domain or publicly regulated from the late 19th century onward. The premier example of this is the French *Crédit Mobilier* bank founded by followers of the Count de Saint-Simon (1760–1825), who inspired key Classical economists including Karl Marx and John Stuart Mill. The *Crédit Mobilier* bank, founded in 1852, was named in contrast to the common mortgage bank (*Sociétés du Crédit Foncier*) or land banks, which lent money on the security of immovable property. The *Crédit Mobilier* aimed to loan to the owners of movable property and so to promote industrial enterprise, mining and the construction of railways and other infrastructure. Today, the bulk of bank lending is again to real estate and other property already in existence, not for the creation of new productive capacity and innovation of production processes. We need *Crédit Mobilier* – type financial institutions.

b) Tax policy (taxing land and natural resources). Here the foremost Classical-era name is Henry George (1839-1897). In his Progress and Poverty (1879) he observed that much of the wealth created by social and technological advances is captured by landowners and other monopolists via economic rents. This concentration of 'unearned' income – which strictly speaking is not income, though it is a revenue stream – in the hands of the few is, according to George, the cause of increasing poverty precisely in those areas which are more developed. The plight of the poor in the mature economy of New York struck him as much worse than the living standards of the poor in his native (then underdeveloped) California. Today, the impoverishing rent flows are (a) in payment for inflated assets prices and (b) in servicing loans against those assets. A large part of the economy's surplus flows to the property and finance sectors in payment of loans, interest and fees for the use of land and housing. And today just as in George's days, inequality has increased strongly as bank loans have been reoriented away from supporting the real sector and towards FIRE sector loans. This drives up asset prices and thus mortgages, increasing the drain from the real economy while enriching assets owners.

c) Regulatory policy to keep the prices charged by natural monopolies such a railroads, power and gas companies in line with actual production costs plus normal profit. The classical example of this is the US Sherman Antitrust Act (1890), enacted in response to the development of business conglomerates or 'trusts' in the last third of the 19th century, which often stifled competition and manipulated prices. Today again the global financial market place is dominated by a few giants; and in most economies three of four banks control 80% or more of domestic markets. The result is just the behavior that progressive Americans deplored in 19th century business, now played out in finance: artificial price increases for bank services and banker's remuneration, far above the level necessary to cover costs with a reasonable profit left; block buying and price fixing in the trading of financial products; and even fraud and intimidation of competitors. And after the crisis, small banks have been bankrupted in their hundreds while the large banks have been bailed out. Re-introduction of financial anti-trust policies will not be the end (in the first 10 years of existence of the Sherman Antitrust Act, many more actions were brought against unions than against big business). But it will be a start.

5. How the FIRE sector operates

The financial sector has become the leading *rentier* sector. Its 'product'
is debt claims *on* the 'real' economy, underwriting, and money
management on a fee basis. For this it receives interest and
dividends from real estate and business borrowers, and from
consumers. Over time, a real estate buyer typically pays more in
interest to their mortgage lenders than the original purchase price paid to
the property seller.

In its interactions with the government, the financial sector buys bonds
(and also makes campaign contributions). The Federal Reserve pumps
money into the banking system by purchasing bonds and, when the
system breaks down, makes enormous bailout payments to cover the
bad debts run up by banks and other institutions to mortgage borrowers,
businesses and consumers. The government also enhances the real
estate sector by providing transportation and other basic infrastructure
that enhances the site value of property along the routes. Finally, the
government acts as direct purchaser of monopoly services from health
insurance providers, pharmaceutical companies and other monopolies.
In the other direction, the US Government receives a modicum of taxes
from real estate (mainly at the local level for property taxes), not much
income tax but some capital gains tax in good years.

Fig. 3: Interaction between the FIRE and government sectors

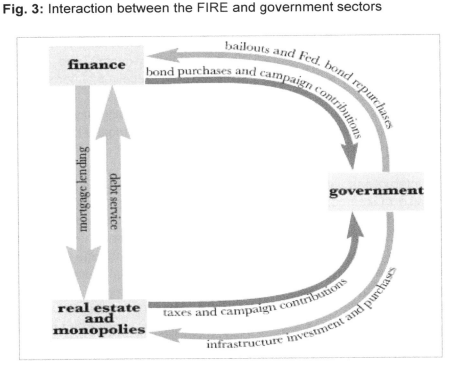

Hardly by surprise, the financial sector prefers to make itself invisible – not only to the tax collector and government regulators, but to voters. In fact, tax polices favor unearned income. The ordinary income tax rate in the US is twice the level of taxes on capital gains: for the 15 % income tax rate brackets, 5-year capital gains taxes are 8%; and for the 39.6% bracket, they are 18% (Kiplinger's, 2009). And yet, since capital gains are not income, higher capital gains tax is opposed on the grounds that this tax falls on (non-capital gains) incomes, which would therefore be unfairly taxed. Minarik (1992, p. 16) writes against capital gains taxation asserting that "the burden of proof should rest on those who would violate the basic principle of equal tax rates on incomes from whatever source". This conflates revenue streams with income.

Successful attempts to break out the *rentier* sector from the rest of the economy – and hence, balance sheet and debt transactions from the purchase of goods and services – have helped soften criticism of shifting the tax burden off land and monopoly rent, and off finance. Yet Epstein and Crotty report that "financial sector total financial assets grew from about a third of total US economy financial assets in the post-World War II decades to 45 percent of total financial assets. Their value was approximately equal to the US GDP in the early 1950s, whereas now it amounts to 4.5 times of the US GDP. Financial sector profit has grown from about 10 percent in the 1950-60s to 40 percent of total domestic profits in the early 2000s".

Fig. 4: Overall model of the FIRE sector: producers, consumers, government, world

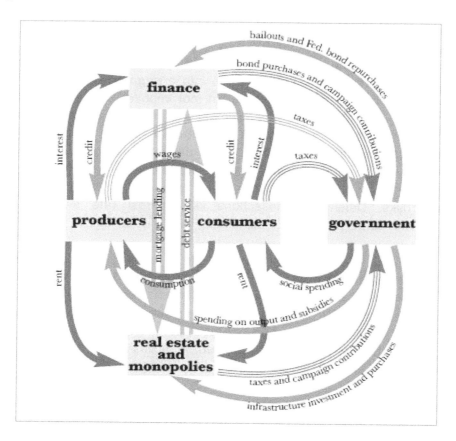

The distinction between *rentier* and 'earned' income was not incorporated into the NIPA. It is as if all income was earned by playing a productive role, and in which money (and hence, credit and debt) were 'neutral', only a 'veil', not as affecting the distribution of income and wealth. Credit was spent only on goods and services, not on assets. And the financial sector's loans always took the form of productive credit, enabling businesses to pay back the loans out of future earnings while consumers paid out of rising future incomes. This is still the representation found in most textbooks today. For instance, Mishkin (2012: pp. 1 and 24) explains that "in our economy, nonbank finance also plays an important role in channeling funds from lender-savers to borrower- spenders... Finance companies raise funds by issuing commercial paper and stocks and bonds and use the proceeds to make loans that are particularly suited to consumer and business needs".

There thus was no explanation of how a credit bubble could inflate real estate prices and then collapse into a negative equity disaster. Finance seemed only to create wealth, not impoverish the underlying economy. Amazingly, this was claimed even for the exotic products whose proliferation preceded the 2008 crash. As late as 2006 academics asserted that "[f]inancial risks, particularly credit risks, are no longer borne by banks. They are increasingly moved off balance sheets. Assets are converted into tradable securities, which in turn eliminates credit risks. Derivative transactions like interest rate swaps also serve the same purpose [of eliminating credit risks, MH & DB]" (Das 2006).

Nor was there any way for mainstream models to distinguish government transfer payments to the financial sector (eg. the $13 trillion in post-2008 financial bailouts in the United States) from Keynesian-style deficit spending. Such transfer payments did not 'jumpstart' the economy. They turned a politically well- connected financial elite into ne vested interests. All this is completely missed in conventional macroeconomics, which cannot come to grips with the role of the financial sector in the economy. Eminent economists have described training in today's macro models as a useless, even socially wasteful activity (Buiter 2009; also Krugman 2009; Solow 2010).

One can understand why the financial sector has had so little interest in tracing the effect of rising money and credit on diverting income from the circular flow between producers and consumers, diverting business revenue from new capital formation, and stripping industrial assets and natural resources. Most model builders isolate these long-term structural, environmental and demographic feedbacks as 'externalities'. But they are part and parcel of reality. So one is tempted to say that the financial element of economic models is too important to be left to bankers and the think tanks they sponsor.

6. Effects on the environment, demography and the economy

Just as debt deflation diverts income to pay interest and other financial charges – often at the cost of paying so much corporate cash flow that assets must be sold off to pay creditors – so the phenomenon leads to stripping the natural environment. The so-called 'debt-resource-hypothesis' suggests that high indebtedness leads to increased natural resource exploitation as well as more unsustainable patterns of resource use (Neumayer 2012, pp. 127-141). This is what occurs, for instance, when the IMF and World Bank act on behalf of global banks to demand that Brazil pay its foreign debt by privatizing its Amazon forest so that loggers can earn enough foreign exchange to pay foreign bankers on the nation's foreign-currency debt. The analogy is for absentee landlords who pay their mortgages by not repairing their property but letting it deteriorate. In all these cases the effect of debt deflation extracting interest is not only on spending – and hence on current prices – but on the economy's long-term ability to produce, by eating into natural resources and the environment as well as society's manmade capital stock.

Demographically, the effect of debt deflation is emigration and other negative effects. For example, after Latvian property prices soared as Swedish bank branches fueled the real estate bubble, living standards plunged. Families had to take on a lifetime of debt in order to gain the housing that was bequeathed to the country debt-free when the Soviet Union broke up in 1991. When Latvia's government imposed neoliberal austerity policies in 2009-10, wage levels plunged by 30 percent in the public sector, and private-sector wages followed the decline (Sommers et al 2010). Emigration and capital flight accelerated: the *Economist* (2010) reported that an estimated 30,000 Latvians were leaving every year, on a 2.2m population. In debt-strapped Iceland, the census reported in 2011 that 8% of the population had emigrated (mainly to Norway).

In as much as investors today have come to aim more at 'total returns' (net income + capital gains) rather than simply income by itself, a realistic model should integrate capital gains and investment into the current production-consumption model. Producers not only pay wages and buy capital goods as in 'current economy' models; they also use their cash flow (and even borrow) to buy other companies, as well as their own stock. When they make acquisitions on credit, the resulting debt leveraging finds its counterpart in interest payments that absorb a rising share of corporate cash flow.

This has an effect on the government's fiscal position, because interest is a tax-deductible expense. By displacing taxable profits, the business revenue that hitherto was paid out as income taxes is now used to pay interest to creditors. The result in the early 1980s when debt-leveraged buyouts really gained momentum was that financial investors were able to obtain twice as high a return (at a 50% corporate income tax rate) by debt financing as they could get by equity financing. This tax incentive for debt leveraging rather than equity investment is the reverse of what Saint-Simon and his followers urged in the 19th century to become the wave of the future.

Conclusion

Only a portion of FIRE sector cash flow is spent on goods and services. The great bulk is recycled into the purchase of financial securities and other assets, or lent out as yet more interest-bearing debt – on easier and easier credit terms as the repertory of bankable direct investments is exhausted. So the pressing task today is to trace how directing most credit into the asset markets affects asset prices much more than commodity prices. Loan standards deteriorate as debt/equity ratios increase and creditors 'race to the bottom' to find borrowers in markets further distanced from the 'real' economy. This increasingly unproductive character of credit explains why wealth is being concentrated in the hands of the population's wealthiest 10 percent. It is the dysfunctional result of economic parasitism.

Keynes recognized a 'leakage' in the form of saving (specifically, hoarding). But at the time he wrote in the midst of the Great Depression there was little motivation to focus on debt service, or on the distinction between direct capital investment (tangible capital formation) and financial securities speculation or real estate speculation (which had all but dried up as asset markets were shrinking to reflect the economy's shrinking). Saving took the form of non-spending, not of paying down debt. There was little lending under depression conditions.

Today's post-bubble attempts to incorporate balance-sheet analysis into NIPA statistics on current activity are too crude. Stock averages do not give an adequate quantitative measure distinguishing the flow of funds into land and capital improvements or industrial capital formation in contrast to speculation in financial securities. So monetary analysis needs to be reformulated along with a better structural breakdown of NIPA to distinguish between money and credit spent on goods and services from that spent on financial assets and debt service.

References

Buiter, W (2009), The unfortunate uselessness of most 'state of the art' academic monetary economics. *Financial Times,* March 3rd.

Cecchetti, S, M Mohanty and F Zampolli (2011), *The real effects of debt.* BIS Working Papers 52, Basel: Bank for International Settlements.

Das, D (2006), Globalization in the World of Finance: An Analytical History. *Global Economy Journal* 6 (1) article 2.

Economist (2010), Far from home: Migration and Latvia. *The Economist,* 1st October.

Epstein G and J Crotty (2012), *How big is too big? On the social efficiency of the financial sector in the United States.* Paper presented at the INET conference, Berlin. Available at www.ineteconomics.org/

Epstein, G (ed.) (2005), *Financialization and the world economy.* Aldershot: Edward Elgar.

George, H (1879), *Progress and Poverty: An Inquiry into the Cause of Industrial Depressions and of Increase of Want with Increase of Wealth, The Remedy.* Garden City, NY: Doubleday, Page, & Co.

Hudson, M (2004), 'The archeology of money: debt versus barter theories of money's origin. In: R Wray (2004) (ed.) *Credit and state theories of money: the contributions of Michael Innes.* Cheltenham UK: Edward Elgar.

Keen, S (2009), Household debt: The final stage in an artificially extended Ponzi bubble. *Australian Economic Review* 42, pp. 347-357.

Keen, S (2011), *Debunking economics: The naked emperor dethroned?* London: Zed Books. Kiplinger (2009), Tax law changes for 2008–2017. *Kiplinger's.*

Krugman, P (2009), How did economists get it so wrong?, *New York Times,* September 6th

Mill, J S (1848), Principles of political economy with some of their applications to social philosophy. Available on http://oll.libertyfund.org/index.php?option=com_staticxt&staticfile=show.php%3Ftitle=101&Itemid=27

Minarik, J (1992), 'Capital Gains Taxation, Growth, And Fairness', *Contemporary Economic Policy*, Volume 10, Issue 3, pp. 16-25, July 1992.

Mishkin F S (2012), *The economics of money, banking, and financial markets.* New York: Pearson.

Neumayer, E (2012), Does high indebtedness increase natural resource exploitation? *Environment and Development Economics,* 10, pp. 127-141.

Obstfeld, M (2009), *International finance and growth in developing countries: What have we learned?* IMF Staff Papers Volume 56, Number 1.

Schumpeter, J (1934), *The Theory of Economic Development.* New York: Harvard University Press.

Solow, R (2010), *Building a science of economics for the real world.* Prepared Statement of Robert Solow, Professor Emeritus, MIT, to the House Committee on Science and Technology, Subcommittee on Investigations and Oversight: 20 July.

Sommers, J D, D Bezemer and M Hudson (2010), The Human Costs of Financial Instability in Latvia. In: D Tavasci and J Toporowski (eds.) *Minsky, Financial Development and Crisis.* Basingstoke, Hampshire, UK: Palgrave MacMillan.

Stockhammer E (2004), 'Financialization and the slowdown of accumulation', *Cambridge Journal of Economics*, 28 (5), pp. 719-741.

Tovar, C (2008), *DSGE models and central banks.* BIS Monetary and Economic Department Working Paper No.258. Basel: Bank for International Settlements.

UNCTAD (2011), *Trade and development report 2012.* Geneva: United Nations Conference on Trade and Development.

Zezza, G (2009), 'Fiscal policy and the economics of financial balances', *European Journal of Economics and Economic Policies*, 6 (2), pp. 289-310.

Finance as warfare

CHAPTER 4

From the bubble economy to debt deflation and privatization

The Federal Reserve's QE3 has flooded the stock and bond markets with low-interest liquidity. This makes it profitable for speculators to borrow cheap and make arbitrage gains buying stocks and bonds yielding higher dividends or interest. In principle, one could borrow at 0.15 percent (one sixth of one percent) and buy up stocks, bonds and real estate throughout the world, collecting the yield differential as arbitrage. Nearly all the $800 billion of QE2 went abroad, mainly to the BRICS for high-yielding bonds (headed by Brazil's 11% and Australia's 5+%), with the currency inflow for this carry trade providing a foreign-exchange bonus as well.

This financial engineering is not your typical bubble. The key to the post-2000 bubble was real estate. It is true that the past year and a half has seen some recovery in property prices for residential and commercial property. But something remarkable has occurred. So in this new debt-strapped low-interest environment, hedge funds and buyout funds are doing something that has not been seen in nearly a century: They are buying up property for all cash, starting with the inventory of foreclosed properties that banks are selling off at distress prices.

Ever since World War II, the operating principle of real estate investors is never to use their own money – or at least, to use as little of their own as possible. Debt leveraging leaves the rental income paid to the banks as interest. The absentee owner is after the capital gain at the end of the bubble's rainbow. That is what a bubble economy is all about. But the only way that investors can obtain current returns above today's miniscule rates is to buy assets directly for cash.

In a bubble economy, falling interest rates (e.g., from 1980 to today) almost guarantee capital gains. But today's near-zero interest rates cannot fall any further. They can only rise, threatening capital losses. That is what is panicking today's bond and stock markets as the Fed talks about ending QE3's near-zero interest rate regime. So there is little incentive for bond buying. Once interest rates rise, we are in an "anti-bubble" economy. Instead of capital gains driving "wealth creation" Alan Greenspan style, we have asset-price deflation.

In the Bubble Economy, families became convinced that the way to build up their wealth was to borrow as much as they could to buy the most expensive home they could, and ride the wave of asset-price inflation. But since 2008, consumers have paid *down* about $5 trillion of personal debt. This has meant using their wages and other income to pay down mortgages, student debt, auto debt, credit-card debt and other bank loans. This leaves only about a quarter of the typical family's paychecks to spend on goods and services after paying the Finance, Insurance and Real Estate (FIRE) sector and the taxes shifted onto wage earners and consumers. The outlook looks dim for corporate sales and hence earnings. So instead of debt-leveraged inflation of asset prices, we have *debt deflation* of the overall economy.

To put this in perspective, from 1945 until interest rates rose to their peak in 1980, there was an almost steady 35-year downturn in bond prices. The Bubble Economy was fueled by interest rates being rolled back down to their 1945 levels and even lower. Credit flowed into the financial markets to buy stocks, peaking in the dot.com bubble in 2000, and then to inflate the 2001-2008 real estate bubble.

So we are now in is the Bubble Economy's *legacy*. We can think of this as Phase 2: repayment time, along with foreclosure time. That is what happens in debt deflation. The Obama Administration has broken its 2008 campaign promises to Congress and to voters to write down mortgage debt to the ability to pay or to market prices reflecting realistic rental values. The debt legacy has been kept in place, not written down.

Carrying this debt overhead has caused a fiscal crisis. The financial and real estate bubble helped keep state and local finances solvent by providing capital gains taxes. These are now gone – and properties in default or foreclosure are not paying taxes. And whereas public pension funds assumed an 8+% rate of return, they now are making less than 1%. This has left pensions underfunded, and prompted some municipalities to engage in desperate gambles on derivatives. But the Wall Street casino always wins, and most cities have lost heavily to the investment banking sharpies advising them.

In place of a new bubble, financial elites are demanding privatization sell-offs from debt-strapped governments. Pressure is being brought to bear on Detroit to sell off its most valuable paintings and statues from its art museums. The idea is to sell their artworks for tycoons to buy as trophies, with the money being used to pay bondholders.

The same dynamic is occurring in Europe. The European Union and European Central Bank are demanding that Greece sell off its prime tourist land, ports, transport systems and other assets in the public domain – perhaps even the Parthenon. So we are seeing a neo-*rentier* grab for basic infrastructure as part of the overall asset stripping.

This is a different kind of inflation than one finds from strictly financial bubbles. It is creating a new neo-feudal *rentier* class eager to buy roads to turn into toll roads, to buy parking-meter rights (as in Chicago's notorious deal), to buy prisons, schools and other basic infrastructure. The aim is to build financial charges and tollbooth rents into the prices charged for access to these essential, hitherto public services. Prices are rising not because costs and wages are rising, but because of monopoly rents and other rent-extraction activities.

This post-bubble environment of debt-strapped austerity is empowering the financial sector to become an oligarchy much like landlords in the 19th century. It is making its gains not by lending money – as the economy is now "loaned up" – but by direct ownership and charging economic rent. So we are in the "economic collapse" stage of the financialized bubble economy. Coping with this legacy and financial power grab will be the great political fight for the remainder of the 21st century.

Finance as warfare

CHAPTER 5

How economic theory came to ignore the role of debt

Starting from David Ricardo in 1817, the historian of economic thought searches in vain through the theorizing of financial-sector spokesmen for an acknowledgement of how debt charges (1) add a non-production cost to prices, (2) deflate markets of purchasing power that otherwise would be spent on goods and services, (3) discourage capital investment and employment to supply these markets, and hence (4) put downward pressure on wages.

What needs to be explained is why government, academia, industry and labor have not taken the lead in analyzing these problems. Why have the corrosive dynamics of debt been all but ignored?

I suppose one would not expect the tobacco industry to promote studies of the unhealthy consequences of smoking, any more than the oil and automobile industries would encourage research into environmental pollution or the linkage between carbon dioxide emissions and global warming. So it should come as little surprise that the adverse effects of debt are sidestepped by advocates of the idea that financial institutions rather than government planners should manage society's development. Claiming that good public planning and effective regulation of markets is impossible, monetarists have been silent with regard to how financial interests shape the economy to favor debt proliferation.

The problem is that governments throughout the world leave monetary policy to the Central Bank and Treasury, whose administrators are drawn from the ranks of bankers and money managers. Backed by the IMF with its doctrinaire Chicago School advocacy of financial austerity, these planners oppose full-employment policies and rising living standards as being inflationary. The fear is that rising wages will increase prices, reducing the volume of labor and output that a given flow of debt service is able to command.

Inasmuch as monetary and credit policy is made by the central bank rather than by the Dept. of Labor, governments chose to squeeze out more debt service rather than to promote employment and direct investment. The public domain is sold off to pay bondholders, even as governments cut taxes that cause budget deficits financed by running up yet more debt. Most of this new debt is bought by the financial sector (including global institutions) with money from the tax cuts they receive from governments ever more beholden to them. As finance, real estate and other interest-paying sectors are un-taxed, the fiscal burden is shifted onto labor.

The more economically powerful the FIRE sector becomes, the more it is able to translate this power into political influence. The most direct way has been for its members and industry lobbies to become major campaign contributors, especially in the United States, which dominates the IMF and World Bank to set the rules of globalization and debt proliferation in today's world. Influence over the government bureaucracies provides a mantel of prestige in the world's leading business schools, which are endowed largely by FIRE-sector institutions, as are the most influential policy think tanks. This academic lobbying steers students, corporate managers and policy makers to see the world from a financial vantage point.

Finance and banking courses are taught from the perspective of how to obtain interest and asset-price gains through credit creation or by using other peoples' money, not how an economy may best steer savings and credit to achieve the best long-term development. Existing rules and practices are taken for granted as "givens" rather than asking whether economies benefit or suffer as a whole from a rising proportion of income being paid to carry the debt overhead (including mortgage debt for housing being bid up by the supply of such credit). It is not debated, for instance, whether it really is desirable to finance Social Security by holding back wages as forced savings, as opposed to the government monetizing its social-spending deficits by free credit creation.

How economic theory came to ignore the role of debt

The finance and real estate sectors have taken the lead in funding policy institutes to advocate tax laws and other public policies that benefit themselves. After an introductory rhetorical flourish about how these policies are in the public interest, most such policy studies turn to the theme of how to channel the economy's resources into the hands of their own constituencies.

One would think that the perspective from which debt and credit creation are viewed would be determined not merely by the topic itself but whether one is a creditor or a debtor, an investor, government bureaucrat or economic planner writing from the vantage point of labor or industry. But despite the variety of interest groups affected by debt and financial structures, one point of view has emerged almost uniquely, as if it were objective technocratic expertise rather than the financial sector's own self-interested spin. Increasingly, the discussion of finance and debt has been limited to monetarists with an anti-government ax to grind and vested interests to defend and indeed, promote with regard to financial deregulation.

This monetarist perspective has become more pronounced as industrial firms have been turned into essentially financial entities since the 1980s. Their objective is less and less to produce goods and services, except as a way to generate revenue that can be pledged as interest to obtain more credit from bankers and bond investors. These borrowings can be used to take over companies ("mergers and acquisitions"), or to defend against such raids by loading themselves down with debt (taking "poison pills"). Other firms indulge in "wealth creation" simply by buying back their own shares on the stock exchange rather than undertaking new direct investment, research or development. (IBM has spent about $10 billion annually in recent years to support its stock price in this way.) As these kinds of financial maneuvering take precedence over industrial engineering, the idea of "wealth creation" has come to refer to raising the price of stocks and bonds that represent claims *on* wealth ("indirect investment") rather than investment in capital spending, research and development to increase production.

Labor for its part no longer voices an independent perspective on such issues. Early reformers shared the impression that money and finance simply mirror economic activity rather than acting as an independent and autonomous force. Even Marx believed that the financial system was evolving in a way that reflected the needs of industrial capital formation.

Today's popular press writes as if production and business conditions take the lead, not finance. It is as if stock and bond prices, and interest rates, reflect the economy rather than influencing it. There is no hint that financial interests may intrude into the "real" economy in ways that are systematically antithetical to nationwide prosperity. Yet it is well known that central bank officials claim that full employment and new investment may be inflationary and hence bad for the stock and bond markets. This policy is why governments raise interest rates to dampen the rise in employment and wages. This holds back the advance of living standards and markets for consumer goods, reducing new investment and putting downward pressure on wages and commodity prices. As tax revenue falls, government debt increases. Businesses and consumers also are driven more deeply into debt.

The antagonism between finance and labor is globalized as workers in debtor countries are paid in currencies whose exchange rate is chronically depressed. Debt service paid to global creditors and capital flight lead more local currency to be converted into creditor-nation currency. The terms of trade shift against debtor countries, throwing their labor into competition with that in the creditor nations.

If today's economy were the first in history to be distorted by such strains, economists would have some excuse for not being prepared to analyze how the debt burden increases the cost of doing business and diverts income to pay interest to creditors. What is remarkable is how much more clearly the dynamics of debt were recognized some centuries ago, before financial special-interest lobbying gained momentum. Already in Adam Smith's day it had become a common perception that public debts had to be funded by tax levies that increased labor's living costs, impairing the economy's competitive position by raising the price of doing business. The logical inference was that private-sector debt had a similar effect.

How national debts were seen to impair economic competitiveness prior to Ricardo

An important predecessor of Adam Smith, the merchant Mathew Decker, emigrated from Holland to settle in London in 1702. In the preface to his influential *Essay on the Causes of the Decline of the Foreign Trade*, published in 1744, he attributed the deterioration in Britain's international competitiveness to the taxes levied to carry the interest charges on its public debt. These taxes threatened to price its exports out of world markets by imposing a "prodigious artificial Value . . . upon our Goods to the hindrance of their Sale abroad." Taxes on food and other essentials pushed up the subsistence wage level that employers were obliged to pay, and hence the prices they had to charge as compared to those of less debt-ridden nations.

The tax problem thus was essentially a debt problem, which in turn reflected royal military ambitions. Eight centuries of warfare with France had pushed Britain deeply into debt. Interest on the government's bonds was paid by levying excise taxes that increased prices. The cost of doing business was raised further by the high prices charged by the trading monopolies such as the East India Company (of which Decker himself had been a director) that the government created and sold to private investors for payment in its own bonds.

The system of funding wars by running into debt rather than on a pay-as-you-go basis was called Dutch Financing because, as Adam Smith explained (*The Wealth of Nations*, V, iii; Cannan ed.: 452), "the Dutch, as well as several other foreign nations, [have] a very considerable share of our public funds." In fact, they held more than half of these securities, including shares in major Crown corporations such as the East India Company and Bank of England, on which Britain paid a steady flow of interest and dividends that absorbed much of its trade surplus. "As Foreigners possess a Share of our national Funds," Smith wrote (anticipating the complaint of global debtors ever since), "they render the Public in a Manner tributary to them, and may in Time occasion the Transport of our People, and our Industry."

The economic popularizer Malachy Postlethwayt estimated that Seven Years War (1757-63) cost Britain £82 million. In the year the conflict broke out, his pamphlet on *Great-Britain's True System* (1757:165) explained how the taxes levied to service the public debt had increased the nation's cost structure: "the Sum-Total of these Taxes is at least 31 per Cent. of the annual Expense of the whole People of England. Now, where is the Nation with which we can enter into a Competition of Commerce on equal Terms? And what Matter is the 1 or 2 per Cent. Advantage we boast over some of our Rivals in the interest of Money, towards restoring the Equality between them and us?"

The economy's financial problem was whether to lend its savings to the government (almost exclusively to finance wars) or invest them in industry and commerce. "The more the Nation runs into Debt," Postlethwayt warned (*ibid.*:20f.), "the more Money will be locked up in the Funds, and the less will there be employed in Trade." Taxing the population to pay interest to public creditors would drain money that otherwise could be used to fund private investment. "Before such Debt took Place, every body possessed their whole Gains," he added (pp. 52f.). "If the present public Debt instead of being encreased, was paid off, the Profits of the Manufacturers, Tradesmen and Merchants, &c. would be all their own," doubling their rate of profit. "This would be equal in every Respect to a Bounty to that Amount on all our Productions and Fabricks: with that Advantage we should be able to undersell our Neighbours; Our People would of Course multiply; Our Poor would find ample Employment; even the aged and infirm might then earn enough to live upon; new Arts and new Manufactures would be introduced, and the old ones brought to greater Perfection."

Inasmuch as paper credit was convertible into bullion, the outflow of capital and dividends reduced the monetary base for Britain's credit superstructure. This threatened to leave the nation with no wherewithal to employ labor, and hence little domestic market for its own products. Like many of his contemporaries, Postlethwayt (p. 53) decried the remittance of debt service to Dutch investors on the ground that the outflow of bullion led to a monetary stringency, resulting in less production and higher prices. This is just what modern third world debtors have suffered for the past half-century under IMF austerity programs in order to pay their foreign-currency debts.

Even if all the debt were held at home, Postlethwayt warned (p. 21), "it would not upon that account be less pernicious." Taxpayers would pay the bondholders, who tended to spend their revenue unproductively. Even worse: "Funding and Jobbing too often . . . introduces Combination and Fraud in all Sorts of Traffic. It hath changed honest Commerce into bubbling; our Traders into Projectors; Industry into Tricking; and Applause is earned when the Pillory is deserved." He then described what modern analysts call the crowding-out phenomenon (p. 69):

> The national Debts first drew out of private Hands, most of the Money which should, and otherwise would have been lent out to our skilful and industrious Merchants and Tradesmen: this made it difficult for such to borrow any Money upon personal Security, and this Difficulty soon made it unsafe to lend any upon such Security; which of Course destroyed all private Credit; thereby greatly injured our Commerce in general . . .

These complaints seem so modern that one may ask why Postlethwayt has been so neglected all these years. He might have been speaking of today's Latin American and Asian debtors in concluding (pp. 22f.) that Britain's wars and standing armies "hath overwhelmed the Nation with Debts and Burthens, under which it is at present almost ready to sink; and it hath not only hindered those Debts from being paid off, but will daily contribute to enhance them; for while there is more to be got by Jobbing, than by dischargeing our Debts, all Arts will be used to encrease the new Debts, not to redeem the Old." In a similar way the protests by Smith and Decker against the sale of public monopolies anticipated today's complaints that the monopoly profits, dividend payouts and interest charges by the public utilities that Britain sold off to cope with its national debt problems in the 1980s and '90s have increased the costs that the economy's labor and industry must pay.

The great systematizer of mercantilist principles, James Steuart, pointed to many positive results of England's credit/debt superstructure, but acknowledged that "if we suppose governments to go on increasing, every year, the sum of their debts upon perpetual annuities, and appropriating, in proportion , every branch of revenue for the payment of them; the consequence will be, in the first place, to transport, in favour of the creditors, the whole income of the state, of which government will retain the administration" (*Principles of Political Œconomy* [1767]:II, 349ff.).

This actually has become the aim of today's ideology of privatization, which goes hand in hand with an advocacy that planning by financial institutions is preferable to that of government – or more to the point, that interest rates, employment, price and wage targets should be set by the Federal Reserve Board. In view of what has happened to today's debt-wracked economies, such warnings as those of Steuart were prescient. Britain's government was threatened with the prospect of being turned into little more than a collection agent for overseas bondholders and a rising vested financial interest at home.

If public borrowing forced up interest rates and diverted money away from productive investment, agricultural and industrial productivity could not keep pace with the growth in debt-service charges. The implication was that wars eroded rather than built British international power, for the decisive levers in Anglo-French rivalry lay beyond the military battlefield, above all in the financial sphere. Higher debts and taxes threatened to increase Britain's production costs and export prices, impairing its balance of trade regardless of the nation's military victories. Bullion would flow out and industry would stagnate, leaving Britain without the monetary sinews needed ultimately to defend itself against nations growing economically stronger.

Adam Smith's views

Smith's protest against government profligacy and taxation was essentially an argument against war debts. He saw that new wars could be financed only by running further into debt, as populations were unwilling to support them when they had to pay taxes to defray their costs directly on a pay-as-you-go basis and thus felt the full economic burden immediately. The landed gentry, whose members formed the cavalry and officer corps, supported wars out of patriotism but opposed the proliferation of public debts whose interest charges were defrayed by taxes that fell ultimately on their own property. When the barons had opposed royal taxation in medieval times, rulers avoided the tax constraint by borrowing from Italian bankers and other lenders.

By the 18th century, governments had turned to more anonymous Dutch and domestic investors. This created a vested interest of bondholders. And it was only natural for them to portray their lending in as patriotic and economically productive a light as they could, claiming to provide capital to the nation. However, Smith wrote (V, iii; Cannan ed. pp. 460ff.): "The opinion that the national debt is an additional capital is altogether erroneous." Debt was just the opposite of an engine of development. A nation's real wealth lay in its productive powers, not its money or the buildup of financial securities. These were only the shadowy image of real wealth. In fact, Smith explained, the policy of funding wars by bond issues diverted money that taxpayers could use more productively for direct investment. Taxes to pay debt service were "defrayed by the annual destruction of some capital which had before existed in the country; by the perversion of some portion of the annual produce which had before been destined for the maintenance of productive labour, towards that of unproductive labour."

Smith thus joined Decker, Postlethwayt and other critics of the Funding System in observing that public debts forced up taxes to pay interest charges – money that otherwise would be "employed in maintaining productive labour." Whereas industrial and commercial borrowers invested the proceeds to acquire capital whose earnings served to pay off the debt, governments borrowed to wage wars. A deteriorating economic spiral ensued as the taxes needed to carry these debts threatened to "diminish or destroy the landlord's ability to improve his land, and induce the owner of capital to remove it from the country" (pp. 464f.).

By the time Smith published *The Wealth of Nations* there seemed to be little likelihood of Britain paying down her national debt. Tax revenues had become "a fund for paying, not the capital, but the interest only, of the money which had been borrowed . . ." (pp. 450f.). He warned that at some point the burden of war debts would drive the belligerent nation bankrupt, for "Bankruptcy is always the end of great accumulation of debt."

Public bondholders felt little obligation to promote long-term investment for the nations to whose governments they lent money. Although "a creditor of the public has no doubt a general interest in the prosperity of the agriculture, manufactures, and commerce of the country, he has no interest in the good condition of any particular portion of land, or in the good management of any particular portion of capital stock." All that creditors really cared about was the government's power to levy taxes to raise the revenue to pay their debts. When the debt and tax burden had impoverished a country, they could remove their capital to other lands to repeat the process, as has happened again and again.

In sum, the ability of Britain's government to wage war rested on its power to run up debt, which in turn rested on the power to tax. The struggle to free the economy from taxes involved freeing it from public debt, and this required constraints on royal ambitions. Tax charges were not direct production costs, but were the price to be paid for military self-indulgence financed by bonds and other borrowings or the sale of the public domain and monopolies. Such taxes and sell-offs threatened to grow as military technology was becoming more capital-intensive for shipbuilding and cannon, and as the field of conflict with France stretched to America.

In this perception lay the seeds of the economic individualism of Adam Smith and many of his Whig contemporaries. If Britain were to secure a commercial advantage, it would have to reduce the taxes that had been imposed to carry its war debts. This entailed loosening the Old Colonial System so that economic competition would replace military and political coercion.

How Ricardo's value and trade theory ignored the impact of debt and interest charges

The debt discussion peaked at a time before most modern readers imagine that economic theory began. It was the bond-broker Ricardo that ended the discussion rather than moving it forward. His labor theory value focused only on the direct costs of production, measured in labor time. Credit and interest charges did not enter into his model. Workers earned the subsistence wage, and capital was valued in terms of the labor needed to produce it. The land was provided freely by nature, and its natural fertility (and hence, economic rent) was not a cost of production. As for the taxes to which Ricardo referred in his 1817 *Principles of Political Economic and Taxation*, they were the tariffs levied on agricultural products, not taxes levied to pay bondholders. Yet as the economic historian Leland Jenks has observed (1927:14ff.), Britain's government paid out some three-fourths of its tax revenue as dividends to bondholders in the typical year 1783. "Nine million pounds were paid to *rentiers* when the entire annual turnover of British foreign trade did not exceed thirty-five millions."

By 1798, in the wake of the American and French Revolutions, William Pitt's financial policy of borrowing rather than running government on a tax-as-you-go basis imposed interest charges so heavy that, in Jenks' words, "the nation was mortgaged to a new class of society, the *rentiers*, the fundholders , for an annual sum of thirty million pounds, three times the public revenue before the revolutionary wars. The bulk of this sum was being collected in customs, excise and stamp duties, and constituted an engine by which wealth was transferred from a large consuming public to the much smaller number who owned consols," that is, government bonds with no fixed maturity, paying interest only – forever.

Prices for gold and other commodities had drifted upward after the paper pound's convertibility into gold was suspended in 1798. This set the stage for postwar depression after the Napoleonic Wars ended in 1814 and the Bank of England decided to restore the convertibility of sterling currency into gold at the low prewar price level. Debtors had to repay their obligations in money that was becoming more expensive, giving bankers and bondholders a free ride. Seeking to avoid blame, they nominated Ricardo for a safe seat in Parliament to represent their interests.

He set about to convince voters (still made up mainly of property holders) that the nation's economic problems were not caused by debt deflation, but by the Corn Laws, as Britain's agricultural tariffs were called. These high tariffs supported high domestic prices for agriculture on the logic that high food prices would support rental earnings that could be invested to increase output. Over time this would enable Britain to replace imports with higher domestic production levels. But Ricardo argued that higher prices merely would give protected industries a free lunch, above all in the form of land rent, assuming no investment of this revenue to enhance productivity. Ricardian value theory provided a way to measure this unearned income, the element of price that had no counterpart in cost outlays except for the least efficient, highest cost (zero-rent) producers.

Given the subsistence conditions of the day, wages reflected food prices. These in turn reflected agricultural productivity. As Britain's population growth forced resort to poorer soils to produce the crops needed to feed it, producers on the most fertile land enjoyed a widening margin of market price in excess of their own low costs. The marginal supply price was determined by production costs on the least fertile soils, as long as protective tariffs blocked consumers from buying from lower-cost suppliers abroad.

Ricardo portrayed this agricultural cost differential – economic rent – rather than interest as the paradigmatic form of unearned income. It was an element of price that had no corresponding cost of production for well-situated producers. The best way to minimize it, he explained, was for Britain to open its markets to foreign producers, so that high-cost soils would not need to be brought into cultivation. In exchange, foreigners would be asked to open their own markets to British manufactures. Each nation would produce what it was "best" at producing.

This tradeoff became the new objective of British diplomacy, whose market-oriented strategy replaced the Old Colonial System's coercive prohibitions against colonial manufacturing. Underlying this new policy was the perception that if Britain were to undersell its potential rivals to become the workshop of the world, it needed to minimize the money wages it paid its labor. The work force could be fed least expensively by importing grain rather than supplying it with high-cost domestic production. From 1817 through the repeal of the Corn Laws in 1846 the great political struggle in Britain therefore was between the free-trade Manchester School and the protectionist landed interest. In the United States, Germany and other countries the fight was between industrial protectionists and agricultural free traders who hoped to exchange their raw materials for relatively cheap British manufactures.

How economic theory came to ignore the role of debt

Ricardo was the first major economist to be a financier since John Law, who had managed France's Mississippi Bubble a century earlier, in the 1710s. At first glance it seems ironic that a bond broker should have developed classical trade theory in a way that viewed exchange essentially as barter rather than analyzing of how public and private-sector debt levels influenced production costs. Of all people who should have been aware of the financial elements of costing, it would seem that a bond broker would have had a comparative advantage in incorporating such considerations into his trade theory. Yet one looks in vain for a discussion of how debts and the taxes to carry them affected prices and international pricing.

Today, global competitiveness in automotives, steel-making and other capital-intensive industries turns less on wage rates than on variations in the cost of financing investment – interest rates and debt/equity ratios, taxes, subsidies and land or rent charges. Yet such financial considerations do not appear as elements of production cost in Ricardo's value theory, nor do they appear in today's Chicago School monetarism that stands in line with Ricardian doctrine. By focusing on labor-time proportions, Ricardo implied that non-labor expenses such as interest did not really matter. As for taxes, they mattered to the extent that import tariffs forced up the price of labor's food and other necessities, but there was no memory of the long analytic tradition that attributed taxes to the Funding System's interest payments on the public debt. Hence, the policy conclusion of Ricardo's comparative labor-time approach to international trade theory was not that nations should avoid going into debt, but that they should abolish their tariffs to lower prices.

This limited approach implicitly took bond brokers and bankers off the hook from accusations that their debt charges impaired the nation's well being. Ricardo's advocacy of free trade and its consequent specialization of production among countries promised to create a growing commercial loan market and an even larger bond market to finance transport infrastructure such as railroads, canals and shipbuilding.

No prior economist had claimed that public and private debt levels did not affect competitiveness. Yet this is what Ricardo's trade and value theory implied by not acknowledging any impact of debt service or that monetary stringency had to be imposed to stem the drain of bullion to pay foreign creditors. In these respects he was like an individual viewing the world around him, but not seeing himself (or in this case, finance) in the picture. He denied that paying foreign debts had any serious economic impact, depicting them as being self-financing by an automatic monetary adjustment process. This approach rationalized the kind of deflationary austerity imposed today on hapless debtor countries, providing the conceptual foundation for modern IMF and World Bank austerity doctrines.

Inasmuch as money and credit are forms of debt, one would think that monetarists working for central banks, finance ministries and business schools would analyze the debt burden and its interest charges, but they have followed Ricardo's shift of emphasis away from discussing its impact. Yet so powerful was his labor theory of value – powerful largely because of its abstraction, not its economic realism – that it led subsequent generations to speculate about how economies might function if debt and other non-labor costs had no effect on national competitiveness, living standards and the polarization of incomes and wealth.

Europe's 1815-1914 century of relative peace reduced the need for war financing, alleviating concerns about the public debt. The soaring productive powers of labor, capital and land enabled economies to carry higher levels of debt, financed readily by the growth of savings. The financial interests threw their weight behind industry. Opposing the landed aristocracy's Corn Laws, economic theory focused on price competitiveness as determined by labor productivity, using food prices as a proxy for wage levels. Credit was depicted as financing capital formation, headed by public spending on railroads, canals and other internal improvements in Britain and overseas.

Landholders had not yet become a major market for lenders. Except for insiders, personal and mortgage debts were viewed more as emergency measures than as a catalyst to get rich quickly. For all but a few financial operators the practice of debt pyramiding – borrowing money to buy properties steadily in price – would have to await the modern era of asset-price inflation. There was little hint that financiers and real estate interests would join to form a *rentier* bloc. Nobody anticipated the degree to which urban real estate would develop into the banking system's major loan market, in which developers, speculators, absentee owners and homeowners would pay most of the land's net rental revenue to mortgage lenders.

From the critique of economic rent to the critique of property rights of rentiers

Ricardo was the first major economist to portray protectionist landlords as having interests at odds with those of society at large. However, he believed that the rent problem – economic free rides – could be solved and British industrialization put on a firm footing by embracing free trade. His doctrines supported the flowering of trade credit and international investment, which were making quantum leaps forward in his day.

The opposition of Ricardian value and rent theory to Britain's vested interests, the landed aristocracy surviving from Britain's feudal past, made his approach seem progressive. What seems surprising in retrospect is the degree to which landlord spokesmen followed the shift of attention to rent, letting themselves be distracted from the analysis of how debt financing threw the brunt of carrying public spending onto their class.

In pointing out that landlords spent their rental income on servants, coach-makers and other such labor, Thomas Malthus emphasized the role of macro-economic demand, but did not discuss how debt service was deflationary. Defending the Corn Laws, his point was that although landlords and their employees might be unproductive, at least they spent their wages on the products of industry, spurring the domestic market. Ricardo's free trade proposals aimed at supporting industry more directly, by repealing the tariffs that obliged employers to pay their workers high enough wages to cover the nation's highly protected grain prices.

Adam Smith had remarked that landlords liked to reap where they had not sown, he also described their objective as being to promote prosperity inasmuch as they were the major beneficiaries of a thriving economy and growing population. Ricardo agreed that they were its major beneficiaries, but accused them of gaining passively via a free ride – economic rent. He believed that economic rent was caused by fertility differentials inherent in nature, and that nothing could alter "the original and indestructible powers of the soil" responsible for the natural superiority of some lands to others. When Malthus argued that landowners would invest their rental income in the land to improve its yields so as to earn more revenue, Ricardo replied that even if landlords did this, it would not overcome the differentials in soil fertility responsible for causing economic rent. Overall productivity might rise if fertilizer or machinery were applied to the soil, but the yield proportions would remain unchanged! The agricultural chemistry of Justus von Liebig and Thaer soon showed that this assertion was unscientific, but Malthus did not criticize this, nor did he criticize the financial blind spot in Ricardian reasoning. Despite the fact that it was mainly the landlords that were taxed to pay interest on government borrowings, they let the debt issue simply was shelved.

As resentment against the public debt and creditors waned, hostility toward landlords peaked. Yet although Ricardo accused protectionism of increasing rents, he did not challenge the property rights of landlords to receive them. He shifted the economic policy debate away from the interest problem to that of rent, but did not question the property rights of landed *rentiers* any more than those of financial *rentiers*. It was the philosophic radical John Stuart Mill, son of the economic journalist and Ricardian popularizer James Mill, who made a more far-reaching argument against the right of landlords to receive rent that once had accrued to the public domain. For J. S. Mill such rent was the ultimate free ride. He believed that rents (most of which were on inherited lands) should be returned to the public domain as the tax base, as it had been in feudal times.

This brought into question property rights as such, an inquiry that was pursued with the greatest intensity in France, and soon would be questioned even more radically by the Marxists. It was first in France, in the wake of the French Revolution's overthrow of the monarchy and feudal aristocracy, that a more radical challenge to property would be made, including a challenge to the interest collected by the banking families that had emerged to create a new, post-feudal power.

Banking theory and industrialization

Although British banks were all in favor of the flourishing trade that pro-industrial policies promised to bring about as Britain became the workshop of the world, they played little role in developing an industrial credit market. What they had done for centuries was to provide short-term trade credit, discount bills of exchange and transfer international payments. Such lending promised to grow as a result of the global specialization of production that Ricardo's free-trade policies aimed to promote, but that was the extent of matters. Railroads, canals and other infrastructure used the stock and bond markets rather than banks for their long-term funding. Even so, Britain's security markets did not provide its industry with long-term credit to anywhere near the degree achieved by the financial systems developed in continental Europe.

The economic dislocations in all countries after 1815 made it clear that banking and financial structures would determine which nations would ride the crest of the Industrial Revolution. Stepping back to take a broad view of what their nations needed to catch up, it was French and German policy makers that moved banking theory into the industrial age. In France, followers of the Count Claude-Henri de St. Simon (1760-1825) saw that new banking institutions were needed to finance industry, thereby replacing the traditional consumer usury, trade financing and lending to governments. Their theorizing along these lines created a veritable economic religion based on the credit system's role in planning and allocating the resources of industrial society.

In 1821, St. Simon published *Du Système Industriel*. Among the followers he attracted were Prosper Enfantin and Saint-Amand Bazard, whose ideas were summarized in *Doctrine de Saint-Simon, Exposition, Première année* (1828/29). Subsequent admirers included the social philosopher Auguste Comte, the economist Michel Chevalier, the socialist Pierre Leroux, the engineer Ferdinand Lesseps (whose plans for international canals elaborated ideas initiated by St. Simon) and the brothers Emile and Isaac Pereire who founded the Crédit Mobilier in 1852. Outside of France, St. Simon influenced John Stuart Mill, Marx and other socialists.

79

The St Simonians were the market reformers of their day. One even might call them market evangelists, but what made them more fundamentally radical than today's libertarians was the fact that they treated the inequalities caused by inherited wealth as market imperfections to the extent that such power was not earned directly through one's own ability and merit. As an enlightened democratic aristocrat St. Simon saw hereditary privilege as a parasitic burden for society. His 1819 satire *Parabole* depicted the governing aristocracy and *nouveaux riches rentiers* as living easily off their inherited rent and interest revenues rather than playing an active role in promoting industrial development. St Simon's objective accordingly was to replace the hereditary *rentier* class with a regime based on merit.

The basic theme was that talent was best able to show its ability in industry, but it needed credit, and this required a reformed financial system. Paramount among the St Simonian reforms was the principle that credit should be productive, not usurious. Past lending was criticized for indebting the rest of society without putting in place new means of production. To rectify matters governments were urged to coordinate industrial planning so as to provide a productive field for the investment of savings and credit. Each city was to be headed by a mayor acting as *chef-industriel* (head of industry), who would allocate the means of production and set income levels. These banker chiefs were to be appointed by national economic "priests" who would hold ultimate power. In this doctrine lay the seeds of a centralized government *dirigisme*.

A basic issue posed by 19th century political economy was who would allocate resources best – the market or government? It was recognized that every economy is planned by someone or other. The St. Simonians, Marxists and "state socialists" of Bismarck's Germany believed – and indeed, hoped – that financial engineers would become virtual public planners.

The St Simonians proposed a system to operate through financial intermediaries to mobilize and mediate the use of resources. They hoped to transform debt and credit from the burdensome forms imposed by centuries of consumer usury and government war-financing into productive, self-amortizing industrial lending to finance investment in factories, technology and a broad national economic infrastructure. It was expected that as banking and finance were harnessed to serve the industrial imperatives of society, power-driven manufacturing and transport would provide a fertile field for the investment of savings.

Today's world has fulfilled their expectations in the sense that resources are allocated by planners working for commercial banks, investment banks and other institutional investors, while the chief executive officers of major corporations are concerned more with financial strategy than with industrial engineering. Rather than operating as part of government, however, these financial institutions have become vested creditor interests in a way almost the opposite from that hoped for by St Simon. The bankers he envisioned were to be elevated as industry's organizers and promoters. In contrast to the industrial innovators of the sort envisioned by Joseph Schumpeter, the St. Simonians industrial capitalist ("*travailleur*") was a financial engineer, seeing where credit best could be applied to promote physical investment and new technology. According to the compilation *Religion saint-simonienne, Economie politique et Politique* (Paris: 1831:98), "the banks perform the role of capitalists in their transactions with those *travailleurs*, to whom they loan money," enabling these "industrious people" to obtain financing (*ibid.*:45; Marx quotes with approval a series of such passages in *Capital* III [Chicago 1909]:714).

Today's financial management certainly is not unfolding in the way these industrial optimists expected. The planning they endorsed had a long-term time frame based on tangible capital investment, technological innovation, rising productivity and employment. But for today's financial planners the short run effectively has become the only aim. Running a corporation has become mainly a financial task whose objective is to raise the company's stock price by mergers and acquisitions, using earnings to buy one's own equity, arranging debt leveraging and orchestrating global intra-corporate "book" pricing so as to take profits in tax havens. Financial managers are more likely to downsize operations and scale back research and development than to expand employment and production so as to leave more income to pay dividends and interest. The economy's debt burden is made heavier by deflationary policies that keep expansion on a short-term leash, and to encourage rather than tax *rentier* income and debt financing.

This line of development was not foreseen either by the St. Simonians or their contemporaries. Had they anticipated it, they would have depicted it as a financial dystopia.

Emile Pereire took the first steps to put his ideas of an equity-funding system in place in the 1830s, building France's first railway line (running from Paris to St. Germain), followed by other routes. Like Friedrich List in Germany, he recognized the key role of transport in integrating and developing national economies. Such infrastructure needed large financial institutions to provide credit, and in 1852 Pereire formed the *Société Génerale du Crédit Mobilier* as a joint-stock bank designed to direct savings into the stocks of large undertakings. He was joined by his younger brother Isaac, who explained the institution's financial philosophy in *Le Rôle de la Banque de France et l'Organisation du Crédit en France* (1864) and *La Politique Financière* (1879). The aim was to expand industrial production by providing long-term credit at a lower cost than was charged by banking families such as the Rothschilds who monopolized French finance at the time.

To give industry freedom from the constraints imposed by mercantile banking practice, the Crédit Mobilier provided equity capital and bond financing. But this freer supply of long-term credit proved to be its undoing as the bank turned into a pyramid scheme. It borrowed at a low rate of interest and invested in the securities of its customers. When France's economy was thriving this strategy worked, but over the course of every business cycle a downturn comes when stock prices crash. It was at this point that the Crédit Mobilier suffered both as stockholder and as banker, for it had borrowed short and lent long-term. Its deposit liabilities remained fixed in the face of the economic crash that occurred in 1866.

The Crédit Mobilier's close connections with Louis Napoleon's government prompted it to indulge in insider speculation that drove it bankrupt in 1867 and into liquidation in 1871. Rather than making loans the bank invested in the stocks and bonds issued by its customers. "The institution was in effect a gigantic holding company engaged in financing and managing industrial enterprises," notes George W. Edwards (*The Evolution of Finance Capitalism* [1938]:51). "The securities of the controlled companies were used as assets on which the Crédit Mobilier issued its own securities, to be sold to the public. For a number of years the Bank was highly successful, and performed notable service in promoting railroads and public utilities."

Financial scandals plagued the 19th century's largest international investments, headed by the Suez and Panama Canal schemes (both of which had been early St. Simonian ideas), and by America's railway land grants to robber barons whose subsequent stock and bond waterings helped give high finance a bad name. As aggregations of finance capital grow larger and more closely linked to government, banking systems become ingrown and prone to "crony capitalist" insider dealing. There is a reason for this. Savings grow so rapidly at compound interest that savers and investors look for new types of outlet. Inevitably they must lower their standards and lend in an increasingly risky environment, as the risk is aggravated by the volume of debt itself.

By the 1980s, for example, so large a supply of savings had mounted up in the United States that Drexel Burnham's crew of corporate raiders seemed a godsend when they financed their takeovers by high-interest junk bonds. When the dust settled they had left debt-burdened companies in their wake and bankrupted many savings-and-loan associations and cost the Federal S&L Deposit Insurance Corp. (FSLIC) some $300 billion. Japanese insider deals financed a real estate bubble by funneling bank loans to speculators and schemers. The bursting of the Asian Bubble in 1988 showed the extent to which modern financial systems lack the checks and balances needed to direct savings along more productive lines.

Today's market orthodoxy has inverted the 19th-century reformers' spirit by endorsing financial gains indiscriminately. While credit is channeled to create an asset-price inflation, free riders gain wealth not so much by inherited privilege as by their insider contacts with banks. They borrow money to buy real estate and stocks when asset prices are rising, and stick the government's taxpayers with losses when asset prices turn down.

The St Simonian contribution was to emphasize the need for an efficient banking system to provide industry with long-term financing. The school's influence ranged from socialists to German industrialists. As it was not anticipated that finance would overload industrial economies with debt, no one sought to develop a theory to quantify just how much debt economies could afford. No doubt the 19th century's industrial optimists would have been surprised to learn the extent to which today's financial institutions aim not to fund industry but rather to load it down with debt and extract interest. And rather than funding public investment, financial institutions have set about privatizing and dismantling it, stripping away the moral authority with which the St. Simonian reformers, socialists, German bank theorists and other early advocates of industrial progress imbued public planning and enterprise.

Marx's optimistic view of industrial finance capitalism

Engels (*Capital* III:710, fn 116) attributed Marx's ideas of how banking and finance were destined to be transformed by the economic imperatives of industrial technology to St Simon, pointing out that Marx spoke "only with admiration" of his "genius and encyclopedic brain." To be sure, Marx criticized St Simon's followers for being utopian in hoping to reconcile capital and labor. Yet although he spoke sarcastically of St Simon's "world-redeeming credit-phantasies," he shared his financial optimism, most explicitly in asserting that the banking and credit system "signifies no more and no less than the subordination of interest-bearing capital to the conditions and requirements of the capitalist mode of production" (*Capital* III:704f.). What made industrial credit different "from usurer's capital" was "the totally changed character of the borrower ... He receives credit in his capacity as a potential capitalist." Industrial credit would free society from the need to rely on the usurers' hoards of the past, and indeed from the short-term financial leash imposed by Anglo-Dutch mercantile banking.

In his 1861-63 drafts for what would become the later volumes of *Capital*, Marx called the banking system "the most artificial and the most developed product turned out by the capitalist mode of production" (*Capital* III:712). Like the St. Simonians, he expected it to become society's means of planning the future, and believed as optimistically as they did that the needs of industry would transform the shape of lending and investment to finance capital formation on a global scale.

Underlying this view was the perception that there are two ways for a loan to be repaid. If the proceeds are invested to produce a profit, borrowers can pay out of the revenue they earn; otherwise they must reduce their consumption or sell off their assets. Marx believed that productive lending would become the normal state of affairs, although he was one of the first "business cycle analysts" to describe how financial crises occurred periodically when gluts of unsold output led to collapsing prices and bankruptcies that transferred property from debtors to creditors. "Usury centralises money wealth, where the means of production are disjointed," Marx concluded (*ibid.*:700.). And as the means of production became more centralized, he added (*ibid.*:712), "it must be kept in mind that the credit system has for its premise the monopoly of the social means of production in the hands of private people (in the form of capital and landed property)."

Loan balances doubled and redoubled by usury's own laws – the mathematics of compound interest – which were not rooted inherently in the economy's ability to pay and hence were independent of the mode of production. Interest-bearing debt "does not alter the mode of production, but attaches itself as a parasite and makes it miserable," Marx warned. "It sucks its blood, kills its nerve, and compels reproduction to proceed under even more disheartening conditions."

Marx granted that the old reliance on usurers' credit would survive for "such persons or classes . . . as do not borrow in the sense corresponding to the capitalist mode of production" (*ibid.*:705). The usurious practice that survived from antiquity "does not confront the laborer as industrial capital" but "merely impoverishes this mode of production, [and] paralyzes the productive forces instead of developing them" (*ibid.*:699f.). As long as this form of capital exerted control over governments, industrialization would be thwarted and public revenue would be diverted to parasitic forms of finance, limiting the growth of markets by siphoning off labor's wages to pay interest on consumer purchases or other pressing needs. Distress borrowers would pledge (and in due course, forfeit) their collateral.

Anticipating the arguments of Keynes in the 1930s, Marx criticized the Ricardian bullionists for demanding that governments protect the value of loans by imposing monetary deflation. This would stifle the market needed to call forth new investment. "The value of commodities is therefore sacrificed, for the purpose of safeguarding the phantastic and independent existence of this value in money," he warned (*ibid.*:607). "As money-value it is secured only so long as money itself is secure. For the sake of a few millions of money many millions of commodities must therefore be sacrificed," along with new investment and hiring.

Nonetheless, he believed, the jockeying for position between financial and industrial capital would be settled in industry's favor in the end. "This violent fight against usury, this demand for the subordination of the interest-bearing under the industrial capital," Marx promised (*ibid.*:707), "is but the herald of the organic creations that establish these prerequisites of capitalist production in the modern banking system. The hard-money age of usury no longer would deter society from achieving its technological potential." The financial achievement of industrial capitalism would be to mobilize banking and finance as the tool of industry, creating new institutions to supply industrial credit on the basis of calculations of the borrower's ability to invest the loan proceeds profitably enough to pay the loan with its interest charges. By providing productive credit, the new industrial banking system "robs usurer's capital of its monopoly by concentrating all fallow money reserves and throwing them on the money-market, and on the other hand limits the monopoly of the precious metals themselves by creating credit-money."

If economies were to avoid systemic crisis, they would have to carry the burden of financial claims accruing at compound interest, but Marx believed that industry's productive forces would be up to the task. So did most observers. Captains of industry were expected to steer the ship of state while industrial engineers would do the planning. Rather than watering stocks to load down enterprises with "fictitious capital" and ruining the world's colonial regions as they had done in Egypt and Persia, financiers would coordinate global industrialization. In the end, finance would adjust itself to the underlying "real" economy, becoming a subordinate and derivative layer. Future wealth creation would take the form of building up society's means of production and employment, not merely inflating stock market prices ("paper wealth").

The post-classical reaction analyzes interest without examining money, credit or debt

Classical economics was inherently political by virtue of dealing with society's most basic dynamics. The labor theory of value isolated economic rent as constituting unearned income, an element of pricing that represented a free lunch rather than a cost element remunerating productive effort. To the extent that rent and interest could not be a bona fide production costs, they were brought under fire as appropriate sources of taxation or outright nationalization of the *rentier* claims and property rights that produced them. These policy conclusions made it inevitable that an individualistic and anti-government reaction would arise against the reformist spirit of J. S. Mill as a halfway house to the revolutionary conclusions of Marx.

The first major shots were fired in 1871, by Anton Menger in Austria and Stanley Jevons in Britain. Looking at the economy from a psychological vantage point that placed consumers rather than employers and businesses at the center, the Austrian individualists and British utilitarians based their essentially microeconomic perspective on consumers choosing what products to buy and whether to consume them in the present or defer their gratification to the future in exchange for interest.

The logical method was that of *ceteris paribus*, "all other things remaining equal." This created a world in which consumer utility, saving and interest were discussed as if all other elements of the economic system remained unchanged. By ignoring the economy-wide feedback of given actions, this approach made it possible to avoid thinking about the financial dynamics that shaped the 19th and early 20th century.

The psychological theory, for instance, discussed interest rates as reflecting the degree of impatience to consume goods in the present rather than in the future, without reference to the interaction between interest rates, exchange rates, prices and the magnitude of debt. William Nassau Senior's "abstinence" theory represented interest as payment for a sacrifice on the part of savers, a "factor return" to reward them for the "disutility" or "service" of not consuming their income on the spot but deferring their gratification. Everything appeared to be a matter of choice, not contractual necessity or economic need. The implication was that money was something concrete to be lent out. No reference was made to how credit was created or to the forfeiture of property that ensued when things went wrong. Yet the world's economies were being shaped by "things going wrong," that is, not according to the neat textbook models.

If credit could be created at will, there would be no need for abstinence. Banks were corporate institutions, and had no psychology to consume, but a legal charge to accumulate profits without any diminishing psychic utility. A financially based theory would have focused on the banking system's credit creation and on the fact that governments were their major borrowers and Treasury bonds dominated financial markets and formed the banking system's reserves. It was for purely political reasons that they borrowed from domestic *rentiers* – owing most to the wealthiest ranks of the population – rather than taxing wealth more heavily or simply monetizing public debts.

No gunboats appeared in this theorizing to enforce a creditor-oriented international diplomacy, nor were railway stock and bond waterings recognized. There was no coercion of debtors or no unearned free lunch for *rentiers* and stock jobbers. Such considerations went beyond the measuring rod of utilitarian psychology, having disappeared into the miasma of *ceteris paribus*.

Adam Smith estimated that businessmen operating with borrowed funds would pay half their profits to their backers as interest. The interest rate thus would be half the rate of gross profit prior to interest charges. A century later the Austrian economist Eugen von Böhm-Bawerk reversed the causality and made profit rates depend on the rate of interest. He pointed out that businessmen would not tie up their money in a venture unless they could make more by investing in time-taking "roundabout" production techniques than they could make simply by lending out their money. On this basis the primary return to industrial and finance capital alike was interest. Profit reflected the time needed to plan and put in place complex capital investments, factoring in the time process by discounting investments at the rate of interest.

In the 1930s the Chicago economist Frank Knight explained that interest yields for business represented the risk premium over and above the basic interest rate offered by risk-free bonds. Interest thus was made primary, profit secondary rather than the system's key dynamic as had been the case in classical political economy.

These theories of consumer preference for current over future consumption and other psychological or profit-rate considerations did not require a discussion of the financial system, its volume of debt and the impact of its carrying charges on economic activity. To avoid taking into account the phenomena of inflation and deflation, the evolution and polarization of wealth, and the ways in which debt service affects market demand and commodity prices, neoclassical economists discussed production and consumption as if people lived in a debt-free barter economy. Absolute values were lost sight of, as everything became a matter of ratios and proportions. As Keynes described the new orthodoxy: "Most treatises on the principles of economies are concerned mainly, if not entirely, with a real-exchange economy; and – which is more peculiar – the same thing is largely true of most treatises on the theory of money."[1]

Money was treated not as a political institution (*e.g.* to enable governments to pay their debts) but as a commodity whose value (and hence, the economy-wide measure of prices) was determined by supply and demand. This assumed that money was a fixed volume that could easily be defined. Credit made little appearance. However, Keynes warned, it would be a

---

[1] "A Monetary Theory of Production" [1933], in *The Collected Writings of John Maynard Keynes* 13: *The General Theory and After* (London 1973):409f. Along these lines Keynes criticized Alfred Marshall for stating explicitly in his 1890 *Principles of Economics* (pp. 61f.) "that he is dealing with *relative* exchange values. The proposition that the prices of a ton of lead and a ton of tin are £15 and £90 means no more to him in this context than that the value of a ton of tin in terms of lead is six tons . . . 'We may throughout this volume,' he explains, 'neglect possible changes in the general purchasing power of money. Thus the price of anything will be taken as representative of its exchange value relative to *things* in general' [Keynes's italics]. . . . In short, though money is present and is made use of for convenience, it may be considered to cancel out for the purposes of most of the general conclusions of the *Principles*."
If money is ignored, then so are savings, debts and their carrying charges. The role of money as a medium in which to pay debts is missed entirely, as is the monetization of debt in the form of free credit creation.

dangerous mistake for economists "to adapt the hypothetical conclusions of a real wage economics to the real world of monetary economics." The kind of thinking that underlay "real-exchange economics . . . has led in practice to many erroneous conclusions and policies" as a result of "the simplifications introduced. . . . We are not told what conditions have to be fulfilled if money is to be neutral."

If money were not neutral, neither was the debt burden. Yet Milton Friedman theorized that:

> Holders of foreign currencies [such as U.S. dollars] *want* to exchange them for the currency of a particular country in order to purchase commodities produced in that country, or to purchase securities or other capital assets in that country, *or to pay interest on or repay debt to that country*, or to make gifts to citizens of that country, or simply to hold for one of these uses or for sale . . . Other things the same, the more expensive a given currency, that is, the higher the exchange rate, the less of that currency will in general be demanded for each of these purposes.[2] (Italics added.)

The implication is that countries will elect to pay less on their foreign debts as the dollars in which these debts are denominated become more expensive. But in reality they have no choice. It is much the same when debtors have to pay their debts as domestic prices and incomes fall. The debt burden becomes heavier. Countries that try to pay less as the debt burden becomes more expensive to service are held in default and confronted with international sanctions, trade barriers and a loss of foreign markets. Price and income deflation thus not only shifts the proportions around, the basic structure is altered as a result of inexorable debt obligations

---

[2] Milton Friedman, "The Case for Flexible Exchange Rates," *Essays in Political Economics* (Chicago 1953), repr. in Caves and Johnson, eds., *Readings in International Economics* (Homewood, Ill. 1968):415.

Few economists bothered to specify the highly unrealistic conditions that would have to be met in order for monetary and credit disturbances, debt service and asset prices to be neutral. With sardonic humor Keynes observed that "The conditions required for the 'neutrality' of money, in the sense in which this is assumed in . . . Marshall's *Principles of Economics*, are, I suspect, precisely the same as those which will insure that crises *do not occur*. If this is true, the real-exchange economics, on which most of us have been brought up and with the conclusions of which our minds are deeply impregnated . . . is a singularly blunt weapon for dealing with the problem of booms and depressions. For it has assumed away the very matter under investigation." As John H. Williams, Harvard professor and advisor to the New York Federal Reserve Bank on the balance of payments observed: "About the practical usefulness of theory, I have often felt like the man who stammered and finally learned to say, 'Peter Piper picked a peck of pickled peppers,' but found it hard to work into conversation."[3] Such criticisms could be levied with even greater force against economists who ignore the role of debt and the revenue that needs to be diverted to pay debt service.

Economists who recognized that payment of debt service was not a part of the "real" economy but a subtrahend proposed that it be excluded from national income and product accounts altogether. Alfred C. Pigou reasoned in *The Economics of Welfare* (1920) that these accounts should exclude income "received by native creditors of the State in interest on loans that have been employed 'unproductively,' *i.e.*, in such a way that they do not, as loans to buy railways would do, themselves 'produce' money with which to pay the interest on them. This means that the income received as interest on War loan – or the income paid to the State to provide this interest – ought to be excluded." One wonders what Pigou might have said about the American practice of railroad directors issuing bonds to themselves gratuitously with no real quid pro quo. "Watering the stock," it was called.

Excluding debt service from the statistics meant that its deflationary impact on incomes and prices – that is, the diversion of revenue from the production

---

[3] John H. Williams, "The Theory of International Trade Reconsidered" (1929), repr. in *Postwar Monetary Plans and Other Essays*, 3rd ed. (New York: 1947):134f.

and consumption processes to pay debt service – could not be measured. The degree to which this debt service interfered with Say's law got lost.

The limited scope of analysis suggested by Pigou's definition of economic welfare would be logical if the aim of economic accounts were just to trace the growth of output and consumption. But measuring debt deflation – the degree to which debt service absorbed the economy's revenue – requires a calculation of all interest payments. To the extent that *rentiers* spend their interest receipts on consumer goods and capital investment rather than plowing them back into new lending, such spending would appear in the national production and consumption statistics. But this is a relatively small phenomenon, although it is the narrow point on which neoclassical utilitarian theories of interest base themselves. To understand the dynamics of booms and depressions, debt pyramiding and economic polarization between creditors and debtors, it is necessary to take the financial system into account.

Yet his is not what Keynes himself did. He discussed the rate of interest, saving and investment without integrating debt service into his income theory.

How Keynes discussed saving and investment without citing the role played by debt deflation

Keynes distinguished himself in the 1920s by defining the limits that existed to debt-servicing capacity,[4] above all with regard to the Inter-Ally debts and German reparations stemming from World War I. By 1931 he was pointing out that "the burden of monetary indebtedness in the world is already so heavy that any material addition would render it intolerable. . . . In my own country it is the national debt raised for the purposes of the war which bulks largest. In Germany it is the weight of reparation payments fixed in terms of money. . . . In the United States the main problem would be, I suppose, the mortgages of the farmer and loans on real estate generally." He criticized deflationary monetary proposals as threatening to derange the financial superstructure of "national debts, war debts, obligations between the creditor

---

[4] "An Economic Analysis of Unemployment" (1931, repr. 1973:343-373).

and debtor nations, farm mortgages [and] real estate mortgages," throwing the banking system into jeopardy and causing "widespread bankruptcy, default, and repudiation of bonds."

But by 1936, Keynes was concerned mainly with the shortfall in consumption resulting from people's propensity to save. Pointing out that new investment and hiring would not occur without stronger markets, his *General Theory of Employment, Interest and Money* described the solution to lie in getting people to spend more. The countercyclical government hiring that he advocated would lead to budget deficits, which would have to be financed by debt. Yet Keynesian macroeconomics ignored the role of debt and its carrying charges. This was its major loose end, and the blind spot that has led to the most confusion.

Already in 1902, John Hobson's *Imperialism* warned that growing debt levels would lead to underconsumption. Creditors would collect money at home and search abroad for new fields to lend it out at relatively high rates, to less debt-ridden (hence, "younger") economies most in need of public infrastructure and other capital investment. This dynamic, Hobson believed, was the taproot of a new form of imperialism, one that had become financial rather than military in character.

Keynes took exception to Hobson's underconsumptionist views. As late as 1931 he viewed the problem of recovery as one of lowering interest rates to make direct investment more remunerative than buying bonds (1973:356f.). Writing to Hobson, he expressed the hope that lower interest rates also would solve the problem of debt deflation, but admitted that public spending might be needed to fill the gap created by the diversion of revenue to service debts. Hobson's point "that 'money savings may continue to grow faster than they can be profitably invested' would only be the case in the event of the rate of interest failing to fall fast enough," Keynes believed. But if it fell to zero (as happened in Japan in the late 1990s), the only solution would be "more spending and less saving." Hobson reiterated that the rate of interest was only of limited efficacy. "In certain situations of boom or slump its action seems very slight and unreliable."[5]

Keynes came to accept this position five years later, by the time he published the *General Theory*. His description of the liquidity trap helped swing the political pendulum back toward government activism. The new public aim was to use deficit financing to pump enough income power into the economy to replace the purchasing power that debt service and other saving was removing from the private sector's spending stream. In time, Keynesian-type liberalism would call for government spending to employ labor that would spend its income on goods, whose sale would provide profits for industrial investors. "The system is not self-adjusting," he wrote in 1933 (repr. 1973:491), "and, without purposive direction, it is incapable of translating our actual poverty into our potential plenty." Expenditures that pushed the U.S. Government budget $1 billion into deficit in 1931, he told an American audience (1973:356ff.), "are just as good in their immediate effects . . . as would be an equal expenditure on capital works; the only difference – and an important one enough – is that in the former case we have nothing to show for it afterwards." The same was true of war spending, of course.

Keynes understood the financial sector as clearly as any economist of his day, yet he wrote in a way that diverted attention from the deflationary character of debt. Blaming high interest rates for inducing savers to buy financial securities that not find a counterpart in new direct investment, he went so far as to call for "euthanasia of the *rentier*." He criticized Say's Law (that production creates its own demand), but did not make clear what proportion of saving resulted from debt service; that is, he did not distinguish loan repayments from fresh discretionary saving. National income statistics count paying off a debt as "saving," because it is a negation of a negation (debt).

Having spent years emphasizing that debt payments are not a matter of discretion but reflect contractual obligations, Keynes dropped this idea in his *General Theory*. He confused matters by defining "saving" as tangible direct investment in factories, machinery, construction and other means of

---

[5] Letters to Hobson dated Oct. 2 and 14, 1931, in Keynes, *Collected Writings* 13 (1973:330-336).

production. (His use of the word "hoarding" had connotations of money kept in a mattress, but its more prevalent forms were "indirect" investment in securities and debt pay-downs.) The role of debt and debt-service remained the missing link in his theoretical exposition, and it was not noted clearly by his followers in Britain, the United States or other countries.

In a 1934 article Keynes noted that anyone who did not accept the idea that economies adjusted automatically to any external disturbance – in particular to debt problems – was labeled a crank. He placed himself in their ranks, and his *General Theory* acknowledged the writings of the Swiss-German economist Silvio Gesell as representative of this approach. On the other hand, he noted: "The strength of the self-adjusting school depends on its having behind it almost the whole body of organised economic thinking and doctrine of the last hundred years. This is a formidable power. . . . It has vast prestige and a more far-reaching influence than is obvious. For it lies behind the education and the habitual modes of thought, not only of economists, but of bankers and businessmen and civil servants and politicians of all parties."[6]

Keynes acknowledged that he still had one foot in the orthodox tradition. In the end, all he could do was blame economists for not having developed "a satisfactory theory of the rate of interest" to serve as the regulator of saving, investment and employment. But how could this be done, without tracing the effect of interest rates on the doubling times of debts, the economy's ability to pay, and the structural consequences of forfeiture under distress conditions?

How debt and interest rates are autonomous from the "real" economy

Keynes was not the first economist pointing to savings as not being an unalloyed benefit. Marx had described how the "new aristocracy of finance, a new sort of parasites in the shape of promoters, speculators and merely nominal directors . . . demands . . . precisely that others shall save for him" (*Capital* III:519f.). The saving in this case take the form of debt repayment with interest, much as British money lenders advertise that buying a home helps buyers save by building up equity via their mortgage payments each

---

[6] "Poverty in Plenty: Is the Economic System Self-Adjusting?" *The Listener*, Nov. 21, 1934 (repr. 1973:488).

month. The liquid savings of course accrue to the lenders, not the debtors. But it was mainly fringe groups that warned of the collision course between the debt overhead and the "real" economy's production and consumption trends.

From the Austrians through Fisher and Keynes, economists sought to deduce the rate of interest on the basis of consumer utility and capital productivity. Their dream of integrating the determination of interest rates into price and value theory was something like trying to untangle the Book of Revelation. Their search to discover a neat mathematical solution, determinable in advance, culminated in Keynes's attempts to formulate a "monetary theory of production" incorporating interest rates and money. Unfortunately, he was mixing apples and oranges. The source of confusion lay in the notion that money and credit have a tangible, real cost of production that can be factored into a general, integrated theory of production, investment and employment.

In reality no such unified field theory is possible. At first glance it might seem that a "real" cost of interest might be imputed by calculating and pro-rating the administrative and overhead costs incurred by banks and other creditors, taking into account their loss ratios to assign appropriate risk premiums. But an analysis of their income and expense accounts shows how tautological such a measure would be. Salaries and bonuses, dividends and reserve funds or new projects (including mergers and acquisitions) reflect whatever revenue creditors obtain. Such pseudo-costs are after-the-fact, not foreseeable in advance in the sense that labor, materials and capital-goods costs are foreseeable.

The reality is that credit has no cost of production beyond a modest administrative overhead. Interest rates have no determinate foundation in the "real" economy's production and consumption functions, although they intrude into that system's circular flow. Such charges therefore cannot be assigned to labor or other "real" costs of production, but the administered prices for interest and underwriting fees are akin to economic rent, out of which the financial sector's bloated salaries and bonuses are paid.

How economic theory came to ignore the role of debt

The credit system's dynamics are based on the flow of funds and terms of debt repayment that form a system no more intrinsically linked to the economics of production and consumption than is the weather. When the financial and "real" spheres intersect, they do so in the way that comets intersect with the planetary system, sometimes with devastating collisions that abruptly alter trajectories. To extend the analogy to include compound interest, one should imagine the havoc that would be wreaked by comets whose mass was growing by x% in real terms each year, relative to the constant mass of the planets. The chance of crashes increases exponentially under such conditions, and their consequences become larger.

Mathematical sophistication is of little help when applied to what is assumed to be a debt-free economy. Without analyzing the degree to which wages, profits, rents and taxes are burdened by interest payments to creditors, economic theory will be unable to provide meaningful forecasts or policy recommendations. It was on this ground that Keynes chided economists for reasoning as if the world operated on a barter basis. They used *ceteris paribus* methodology to prevent monetary "distortions" from interfering with their analysis of wages, profits and rents, neglecting to add financial reality back into the picture they were drawing. The study of banking and credit was shunted aside into a sub-discipline, to be analyzed in isolation from "real exchange" problems. This missed the point that finance ultimately is more real than barter exchange, as money is the objective of businesses and consumers alike.

Finance and interest cannot be derived from production and consumption functions, but their impact on these functions can be traced, just as the impact of weather can be traced after the fact, but not explained as a product of economic conditions. A credit-based theory of pricing would start with the perception that debt service represents a rising share of the cost of producing and distributing goods and services. Today, the major factors determining international cost differentials are variations in the costing of capital – not only the rate of interest but also debt/equity ratios, loan maturities, depreciation and tax schedules. These are not production costs but are imposed from outside the real-cost system.

Matters are aggravated by the fact that goods and services are sold in markets where debt service absorbs a rising share of the revenue of labor, business, real estate and government. This causes a debt deflation that reduces the economy's ability to buy products, even while rising debt service adds to production costs. No meaningful analysis of demand – or of the degree to which Say's Law applies – can be drawn up without taking the volume of debt service into account.

Ignoring the role of debt leaves it free to devastate the economic system. Beaudelaire famously remarked that the devil would defeat humanity at the point where he was able to convince it that he did not really exist. Financial interests have promoted the idea that money and credit are merely a veil, passively reflecting economic life as "counters" rather than actively steering and planning economies. The study of debt and its effects have all but disappeared from the curriculum. In an academic version of Gresham's Law, the financial sector's approach to the debt problem has driven other perspectives out of the intellectual marketplace. Policy-makers take the financial and banking system for granted rather than discussing what kind of a system best would serve society's long-term development and best cope with debts that grow too large to be paid without fatally polarizing economies between creditors and debtors.

Posing the debt-repayment problem leads naturally into the analysis of what public responses are most appropriate. This line of analysis is anathema to the vested financial interests, and finds little support in academic economic department dependent increasingly on FIRE-sector subsidy.

It trivializes the debt problem to treat it merely as one of finding an appropriately low rate of interest to equilibrate financial supply and demand, consumer preference and profit opportunities so that the loan can be paid out of the productive investment of its proceeds. Most loans are not invested in tangible capital formation that increase the borrower's revenue and hence debt-paying capacity. And even if they were, the problem lies in the inexorable mathematics of compound interest. What needs to be examined is how to cope with the inherent tendency of debts to multiply in excess of the economy's ability to pay.

CHAPTER 6

The use and abuse of mathematical economics[1]

"There are more things in heaven and earth, Horatio, than are dreamt of in your philosophy" (Hamlet, Act I, scene V).

"Whoever enters here must know mathematics." That was the motto of Plato's Academy. Emphasizing the Pythagorean proportions of musical temperament and the calendrical regularities of the sun, moon and planets, classical philosophy used these key ratios of nature as an analogue for shaping order in society's basic proportions. The population's optimum size, the city's geometric shape and its division into equal "tribal" fractions for voting and fighting in the army were mathematically idealized. But there was little quantitative analysis of economic relations, and certainly no thought that unregulated market forces would assure social harmony. There was no statistical measurement of the debts that wracked the Greek and Roman economies, or of overall output, its distribution and value.

We now have such measures, but can we say that mathematics provides the key to understanding the major economic problems of our time? More specifically, has the marginalist and monetarist application of mathematics become so nearsighted as to lose sight of the economy's structural problems?

The education of modern economists consists largely of higher mathematics, which are used more in an abstract metaphysical way than one that aims at empirically measuring society's underlying trends. It is now over a century

---

[1] This chapter, on the use and abuse of mathematical economics, was published in my book *The Bubble and Beyond*.

since John Shield Nicholson (1893:122) remarked that "The traditional method of English political economy was more recently attacked, or rather warped," by pushing the hypothetical or deductive side . . . to an extreme by the adoption of mathematical devices. . . . less able mathematicians have had less restraint and less insight; they have mistaken form for substance, and the expansion of a series of hypotheses for the linking together of a series of facts. This appears to me to be especially true of the mathematical theory of utility. I venture to think that a large part of it will have to be abandoned. It savors too much of the domestic hearth and the desert island.

If today's economics has become less relevant to the social problems that formed the subject matter of classical political economy a century ago, its scope has narrowed in large part because of the technocratic role played by mathematics. This paper asks whether this has been an inherent and inevitable development. Has the narrowing of scope of economics since the anti-classical reaction of the 1870s – the so-called neoclassical revolution of William Stanley Jevons, Carl Menger, and later of Alfred Marshall and his followers, culminating in today's Chicago School – been inherent in the mathematization of economics? Or, does it follow from the particular way in which mathematics has been applied?

What is the proper role for mathematics to play? Is there such a thing as bad mathematical economics? What kinds of problems do its formulations tend to exclude?

Mathematical economics as tunnel vision

A clue to the modern role of mathematical model-building is provided by the degree to which higher mathematics was deemed unnecessary by 18th-century moral philosophy and the political economy that emerged out of it. To be sure, the labor theory of value was formulated in quantitative terms from William Petty through Ricardo and Marx. Britain's political arithmeticians used statistics, as did the German cameralists. The quantification of magnitudes gives concrete empirical expression to one's logic. But statistical calculations of price indices or various formulae for measuring labor and capital costs are a far cry from model-building.

The use and abuse of mathematical economics

What has become the distinguishing feature of mathematical economics is its formulation of problems abstractly in terms of just a few selected functions, excluding all categories that cannot be expressed in its bare equations. Key dimensions of economic life have been neglected that need not logically have been omitted, such as land pricing. Despite the emphasis that Ricardo gave to rent theory, the land nationalization debate stimulated by John Stuart Mill, Herbert Spencer and Henry George, and the central role that Thorstein Veblen assigned to urban land in Absentee Ownership, land-price gains have been ignored by today's price theory. Macroeconomic analysis likewise excludes asset-price gains ("capital gains") from its definition of economic returns.

A significant role of mathematization has been to impose this narrowness on economic analysis. By focusing on how individuals spend their income on consumption goods, or defray such consumption by saving at an interest rate that allegedly reflects their "time preference" schedules, marginalist mathematics diverts the economist's eye away from the methods used to acquire and build up wealth.

The big picture – society's long-term transformation – is excluded from analysis on the grounds that its dynamics cannot be sufficiently mathematized. Reiss has located the appropriate quotation from William Roscher (Grundlagen, pp. 67f.): "some scientists (attempted to) fit laws of economics in algebraic formulae... But, of course, the advantage of the mathematical mode of expression vanishes the more, the more complex the facts to which they are applied become... In every description of the life of a nation the algebraic formulae would become so complicated that they render a continuation of work impossible."

To be sure, there are ways to reason mathematically with regard to national economic development, and even to changes in the economic system. Brooks and Henry Adams suggested applying the idea of phase change that had been developed by the American mathematician Willard Gibbs.[2] But this

---

[2] Henry Adams, *The Degradation of the Democratic Dogma* (New York, 1919), introduction by Brooks Adams. For a discussion of the application of exponential growth to the movement of history, especially the economic applications of energy,

suggestion fell on deaf ears. The concern of modern mathematical economists is not with social evolution and changing the status quo, but with analyzing the workings of marginal phenomena within the existing status quo.

The earliest expounders of economic relationships in terms of abstract mathematical functions were virtually ignored in their own day primarily because political economy had not yet narrowed into individualistic consumerism or technocratic business planning. It remained an extension of moral philosophy and public policy-making. The technical problems with which the early mathematical economists dealt, such as psychological utility and price formation based on supply and demand, were still far from being deemed to be the highest concern. The marginalists would make a true breakaway by viewing the consumer rather than the producer/employer as the focal point of the economic system, and discussing the economy more from the vantage point of individual psychology than from that of national industrial and financial transformation.

The early mathematical economists concerned themselves with narrower topics such as price formation, business cost accounting and railroad planning. Gossen's mathematical formulation of utility theory was not widely noticed precisely because he focused on problems hitherto considered too mundane to be deemed an essential part of political economy's core. Likewise, von Mangoldt's editor Kleinwaechter disparaged his mathematical illustration of the principles of price formation as "redundant ballast" in view of the fact that no statistical quantification was applicable. He expunged von Mangoldt's graphic examples altogether.

As for Wilhelm Launhardt's railway economics, it was considered too technical to be classified as political economy proper. His analysis did not deal with how railroads reduced transport costs, thereby benefiting the locational value of farmland, residential and commercial property along the trackway, making fortunes for real estate speculators. As any urban planner knows, this "external" effect of railways on land prices is so large as to overwhelm the narrow direct economies involved.

---

see William H. Jordy, *Henry Adams: Scientific Historian* (New Haven: Yale University Press, 1953).

The use and abuse of mathematical economics

Early applications of mathematical notation and graphs to economic problems thus were ignored largely because they were deemed to be more in the character of engineering or merely technical business analysis than full-fledged political economy. The most essential concerns of political economy and German Nationaloekonomie were not amenable to streamlining in mathematical form. And indeed, while today's mathematical economics serves technocrats and financial strategists, it imposes a nearsighted perspective that distracts attention from what formerly was most important, in order to focus on what is merely marginal. In this sense economics has been overly distilled into the microeconomics of price theory, along with a rough macroeconomic income and output statement.

This is not to say that the building blocks of classical political economy could not be expressed quantitatively. The concept of rent served as a measure of unearned revenue by defining it as the excess of price over cost-value. Diminishing returns (or for the American protectionists, increasing returns) could be formulated mathematically, as could the productivity advantages of high-wage labor. What could not be treated with the mathematics then at hand was the political resolution of long-term structural strains. No chaos theory yet existed to deal with broad quantum leaps that occurred as political and institutional changes were introduced from outside the economic system. And as far as the dynamics of history were concerned, no mathematical formula could express the broad range of complexities that literary exposition could provide.

What made political economy the queen of the social sciences in the 19th century was its focus on the transformation of nations. It dealt with the policies most appropriate for their long-term social evolution – their legal and institutional structure, technology and financial organization. At issue was how economic institutions should be improved. The ceteris paribus methodology of marginalism did not deal with such broad contextual issues. It presupposed that the social structure remained constant, and then implied that no change was needed, as economies would respond to disturbances automatically by settling at a new equilibrium. Such an approach does not have much appeal to social reformers, environmentalists, political regulators or historians dealing with the structural aspects of economic development.

Marxism emerged as the preeminent alternative to the emerging marginalist economics largely because it was almost the sole survivor of classical political economy. In addition to retaining the classical breadth of scope and the idea of stages of development, Marx used irony and the idea of inner contradictions as a logical method of interpreting economic history. This was not a method that could well be expressed mathematically. Although Marx used arithmetic examples to illustrate the rates of profit and surplus value for enterprises employing differing proportions of labor and capital, this was not a mathematical model of the economy. The Communist Manifesto hardly could be expressed in mathematical formulae, and no Marxist tried to express dialectical materialism mathematically.

It has taken a hundred years to drive out what formed the most vital concerns of classical political economy: the shape of social evolution, the strains it tends to develop and the indicated responses by the state. As long as these concerns remained paramount, there would be little reason to celebrate the first users of mathematical functions as having made a great breakthrough. Their "discovery" would have to await the time in which economics narrowed its scope and dropped its concerns with long-term transformation.

The role of political economy in the 19th century was precisely to indicate the most appropriate policies for self-direction. That is what made it political economy. But as economics became increasingly technocratic, it dropped the political dimension. And as it has narrowed and come to take the institutional and political environment for granted, the mathematical formulation of economic functions has come to be used as the criterion for acceptable theorizing. The role of mathematics in fact has been to exclude problems that are more than marginal. A basic condition for regression analysis to be applied, for instance, is a constant social and political environment.

In this way mathematical economics has become the ultimate vehicle to make the policy trivialization of economics politically acceptable, establishing status quo economics as a pseudo-science by virtue of using mathematical symbolism. As Wolfgang Drechsler has quipped, mathematics has helped enthrone irrelevance as methodology. The key aspect of the mathematization of economics has been its logical necessity of stripping away what the new economic orthodoxy sought to exclude from the classical curriculum: the socially sensitive study of wealth, how it is acquired, and how its distribution (indeed, its polarization) affects social development.

The semantics of mathematical equilibrium theory

If mathematics is deemed to be the new language of economics, it is a language with a thought structure whose semantics, syntax and vocabulary shape its user's perceptions. There are many ways in which to think, and many forms in which mathematical ideas may be expressed. Equilibrium theory, for example, may specify the conditions in which an economy's public and private-sector debts may be paid. But what happens when not all these debts can be paid? Formulating economic problems in the language of linear programming has the advantage of enabling one to reason in terms of linear inequality, e.g., to think of the economy's debt overhead as being greater than, equal to, or less than its capacity to pay.

An array of mathematical modes of expression thus is available to the economist. Equilibrium-based entropy theory views the economy as a thermodynamic system characterized by what systems analysts call negative feedback. Chaos theories are able to cope with the phenomena of increasing returns and compound interest, which are best analyzed in terms of positive feedback and intersecting trends. Points of intersection imply that something has to give and the solution must come politically from outside the economic system as such.

What determines which kind of mathematical language will be used? At first glance it may seem that if much of today's mathematical economics has become irrelevant, it is because of a fairly innocent reason: it has become a kind of art for art's sake, prone to self-indulgent game theory. But almost every economic game serves to support an economic policy.

Broadly speaking, policies fall into two categories: laissez faire or interventionist public regulation. Each set of advocates has its own preferred mode of mathematical treatment, choosing the approach that best bolsters their own conclusions. In this respect one can say that mathematics has become part of the public relations apparatus of policy-makers.

The mathematics of socialism, public regulation and protectionism view the institutional environment as a variable rather than as a given. Active state policy is justified to cope with the inherent instability and economic polarization associated with unregulated trade and financial markets. By contrast, opponents of regulation select a type of equilibrium mathematics that take the institutional environment for granted and exclude chronic instability systems from the definition of economic science, on the ground that they do not have a singular mathematical solution. Only marginal problems are held to be amenable to scientific treatment, not quandaries or other situations calling for major state intervention.

Marginalist mathematics imply that economic problems may be solved merely by small shifts in a rather narrow set of variables. This approach uses the mathematics of entropy and general equilibrium theory to foster the impression, for instance, that any economy can pay almost all its debts, simply by diverting more income from debtors to creditors. This is depicted as being possible without limit. Insolvency appears as an anomaly, not as an inevitability as in exponential growth models.

Looking over the countries in which such theorizing has been applied, one cannot help seeing that the first concern is one of political philosophy, namely, to demonstrate that the economy does not require public regulation to intervene from outside the economic system. This monetarist theory has guided Russian economic reform (and its quick bankruptcy) under Yeltsin and his oligarchy, as well as Chile's privatization (and early bankruptcy) under Gen. Pinochet, and the austerity programs (and subsequent bankruptcies and national resource selloffs) imposed by the IMF on third world debtor countries. Yet the reason for such failures is not reflected in the models. Empirically speaking, monetarist theory has become part of the economic problem, not part of the solution.

The subjectivity of statistical categories

Political economy developed out of a different tradition from statistics. The word "statistics" itself derives from "state," and early statistics accordingly dealt with public finances, debt and the economy's tax-paying capacity. The focus was on the ruler's fiscal ability to tax the economy and to finance deficits (mainly in times of war) through public debt. From this primary concern rulers developed an interested in how to make their economies richer, so that they could generate more public revenue. This study was called Political Arithmetic. To the extent that laissez faire policies were advocated, it was as an economic plan to encourage economic growth and hence to enhance the ruler's power to tax.

Classical political economy developed largely out of the anti-royalist political ideology of the French Physiocrats and Adam Smith opposing government regulations and taxation. The emerging individualistic discipline came to define the statistical categories that shaped peoples' quantitative perception of economic phenomena.

Accounting formats require a theoretical conceptual apparatus. Categories must be defined before actual statistics can be collected. Any set of categories is itself a conceptual structure of the parts that make up the overall picture. Empirical statistics thus reflect theoretical accounting categories, for better or worse. To mathematize economic models using obsolete or dysfunctional concepts hardly can be said to be scientific, if we define science as the understanding of how the world actually works.

It is difficult to see where economies are generating wealth without dividing their activities into the classical categories of productive vs. unproductive, i.e., wealth-creating labor vs. economic overhead. Unfortunately, few economists remember the great debate over this issue that lasted for over a century.

A case in point is the GNP accounting format developed by Simon Kuznets. Its elements are neither inherent nor entirely objective. All activities are held to be productive, rather than some (such as crime prevention, medical treatment, environmental cleanup costs and warfare) being in the character of economic overhead. The production and sale of cigarettes is counted as output, and the medical treatment of smokers as yet more national product. Crime prevention is counted, but criminal earnings are not reflected in the national income statistics.

On the other hand, the national income and product accounts do not reflect the major way in which the largest sectors – real estate, mining, fuels, forestry, and even banking and finance – take their economic returns, namely, as capital gains. These sectors appear to be operating without earning any taxable profit, and their capital gains are not traced. The accumulation of real estate fortunes and stock-market gains have become the way in which wealthy people, and money managers and homeowners have built up their wealth. But this distinguishing financial phenomenon of the present decade – asset-price inflation – is lost from view by formats that treat capital gains as "external" to their model of how the economy works.

Today's national-income concept of saving gives the appearance that at the end of 1998 the domestic U.S. saving rate was a negative 2 percent of national income. Yet savings are being built up at an unprecedented rate. The low statistical rate of savings simply reflects the high degree to which new savings find their counterpart in debt (including loans to real estate and stock market speculators seeking the afore-mentioned capital gains), rather than being invested directly in the form of new tangible capital..

Meanwhile, a rising proportion of liquid savings is coming from the world's criminals and kleptocrats. Yet national income statistics neglect the economic role played by crime, fraud and other illegal activities, despite their important economic role in generating many of society's major new fortunes. Only what is socially approved seems to be counted among society's shaping dynamics. (In the 1930s, when Roy Ovid Hall tried to include smuggling and other illicit activities in his balance of payments reports for the U.S. Department of Commerce, he was told sanctimoniously to desist from such behavior.)

What is not seen probably will not be taxed. In the United States, real estate and financial interests have actively discouraged collection of meaningful statistics on land-price gains. Congressmen and government bureaucrats have sought to rationalize the real estate gains of their major constituents and campaign contributors. Today's official statistics attribute so much of the price rise to the inflation of construction costs that in 1994 the value of all corporately-owned land in the United States was a negative $4 billion! (The actual land value of U.S. real estate was over $9 trillion at the time.)

These seemingly objective official statistics only distract attention from the reasons why so large a proportion of the economy's savings is being diverted away from new direct investment into real estate and stock market speculation. The party that suffers most is the government tax collector (and of course, labor, onto whose shoulders the tax burden is being shifted). In this respect, the aim of statistics has been inverted from their original function of informing the state how much can be taxed, to concealing taxable gains from users of modern national income statistics.

Problems, dilemmas and quandaries

Students are taught that economics is about making choices between scarce resources, but when resources really become scarce, economists tend to call it a crisis. Every such problem is stated in such a way as to imply a ready solution. Only marginal problems are recognized, not real dilemmas or quandaries. The idea of "scarcity" is just a "little bit" of scarcity – nothing that a slightly higher price won't cure (for output) or a bit lower wage (for employment problems).

Most economic models postulate that unemployment, for instance, can be solved by appropriate adjustments. "Trickle-down" theories of prosperity accordingly call for reductions in wage levels, while Keynesian theories call for or increased public spending to spur demand. Both approaches view savings as financing investment, which is assumed to take the form of tangible capital formation rather than a stock market or real estate bubble.

The important thing is that no structural problems are recognized, that is, no problems that cannot be solved by marginal quantitative adjustments in incomes, prices and wage levels, the money supply and the interest rate. It is in this respect that the mathematics of laissez faire monetarism are microeconomic, depicting the economy narrowly rather than broadly through the long-distance lens of historical development. The analysis may be valid as far as it goes, but it doesn't go very far, as it formulates problems marginally rather than with an eye for structural reform. Looking for small adjustments, such economics misses the degree to which the economy is losing its flexibility and is structurally rigidifying.

For public relations purposes, policy advocates present their "solutions" in a way that appears to make everyone better off. At least somebody's income is depicted as gaining, as if this automatically makes each inhabitant better off for living in a richer society (richer for whom?). Every solution seems to be a free lunch for the economy at large. What are not recognized are situations in which economies collapse because critical break-even conditions cannot be met. When this occurs, economies face dilemmas or, even worse, quandaries.

A dilemma is a situation in which whatever path or "horn" one chooses, it involves pain and the sacrifice of well-being. Somebody or some social value must lose out. Obstacles present themselves on every side, and if the economy avoids being impaled on one horn, it will fall on the other.

It should be noted that falling on one's face is a state of equilibrium. Death is indeed the ultimate state of equilibrium. So is national austerity and its transfer of property from debtors to creditors, and from domestic governments to foreign institutional investors. But marginalist and monetarist equilibrium economics employ a mathematics that does not recognize the possibility of serious dilemmas developing, or of economies falling into quandaries whose financial and economic constraints prevent technological "real" potential from being realized. The preferred method of mathematical economics is general equilibrium analysis in an environment in which only small marginal disturbances are envisioned, not major structural problems or legal changes in the economic environment.

Economies fall into a quandary when the preconditions for a real solution are lacking. Debtors default on their payments, real estate prices fall, and asset prices for bonds and stocks also fall. Banks are unable to cover their deposit liabilities as the market value of their loan portfolios falls. The government is called on to bail them out by issuing bonds, and to pay the interest charges either by raising taxes or cutting back spending programs. The budget is balanced by selling public enterprises to foreign investors, whose remission of profits and dividends creates a balance-of-payments exchange drain that lowers the currency's exchange rate.

The situation becomes worse as the government borrows from the IMF and is forced to enact an anti-Keynesian austerity program. IMF riots break out, the government falls and a dictatorship oriented to serve global financial institutions is installed, friendly to the capital flight which strips the economy of its resources all the faster. Money-capital flees abroad and skilled labor emigrates as the economy shrinks, with no technological cause indicated in the policy models being applied.

Marginal analysis avoids dealing with such quandaries, and the quantum leaps necessary to escape. It selects a rather narrow set of phenomena (labor and materials costs, the interest rate, income and the pattern of demand) to produce models that show how economies might settle at an equilibrium point if left free from outside political interference. What is missed is the degree to which the world economy is being pushed further and further out of balance.

Mathematical economics as a distraction from economic reality

Is it sufficient atonement that so many economists upon retirement merely give an apology acknowledging that, yes, perhaps their economics have all really been just a waste of time? Upon leaving office, each new president of the American Economic Association gives the expected speech showing that he knows full well it is all just a game, and chastises his colleagues for not being more realistic. But do they not have some obligation to set things right? Or is the problem that they cannot see what has to be done?

Although academic economists hardly have shown themselves to be in favor of free markets in their own life, seeking the insulation of tenured positions and sinecures, they know well where their own money comes from. It comes from their ability to endorse creditor-oriented "free-market" policies and condemn government regulation. This premise has led their mathematical models to focus on how individuals can make money in our pecuniary society, but not how public entities can be better run.

The more libertarian the theory, the more authoritarian the economic pedagogy tends to be, precisely because its reasoning rests on specious foundations. In Pinochet's Chile, Chicago economists showed their intellectual intolerance of a free market in economic ideas by closing the economics and social science departments of all universities save for the Catholic University in which they ruled unchallenged. Consensus was established not through reason, but by removing from the scene all who disagreed with their extremist policies.

Over the past generation, courses in mathematical economics have displaced the traditional courses in economic history and the history of economic thought that might have familiarized students with alternatives to today's monetarist orthodoxy. Equilibrium theorizing has expunged a broad understanding of how economies work, and even the long dynamics of economic history, especially where the dynamics of debt are concerned.

The failure of mathematical economics to analyze our epoch's financial strains suggests that its aim has not really been to explain the world as much as to censor perceptions that imply that the financial status quo is unstable and hence must be regulated. Such findings are not congenial to monetarists in their capacity as the political lobby for the financial sector. By ignoring the problems caused by the growing debt overhead, monetarist orthodoxy has removed economic planning from the democratic political process and placed it in the hands of financial technocrats. The effect has been to create a new (and highly centralized) elitist planning in the world's finance ministries and central banks.

This poses the question of whether the most important phenomena and dynamics are being mathematized. Do today's general equilibrium, monetarist and national income and product models correlate the appropriate phenomena, or do they omit key dynamics?

The use and abuse of mathematical economics

To contemporary economists, mathematics has become the badge of scientific method. But is the use of mathematics scientific ipso facto? To what extent may it be methodologically abused?

Many economists are trained in calculus and higher mathematics without feeling much need to test their theories quantitatively. They tend to use mathematics less as an empirical measuring tool than as an expository language, or simply as a decoration to give a seemingly scientific veneer to their policy prescriptions. Mathematics rarely is used to analyze statistically the financial tendencies working to polarize wealth and income, or how economies change their shape as they grow.

This shape is distorted by the inherent tendency for financial claims – bonds, bank loans and other financial securities – to grow more rapidly than the economy's ability to carry them, much less to pay them off. The volume of such claims tends to grow by purely mathematical principles of self-expansion independently from underlying economic trends in wealth and income, and hence from the ability of debtors to pay. Savers/creditors load tangible capital assets and real estate down with debts that in many cases are not repayable except by transferring ownership to creditors. This transfer changes the economy's structural and, in due course, political shape.

But today's monetarist models foster an illusion that economies can carry any given volume of debt without having to change their structure, e.g., their pattern of wealth ownership. Self-equilibrating shifts in incomes and prices are assumed to enable a debt overhead of any given size to be paid. This approach reduces the debt problem to one of the degree to which taxes must be raised to carry the national debt, and to which businesses and consumers must cut back their investment and consumption to service their own debts and to pay these taxes. The task of economic regulation is reduced to one merely of setting an appropriate interest rate to reflect profit rates and consumer time-preference patterns. An array of measures is selected from the overall credit supply (or what is the same thing, debt securities) to represent "money," which then is correlated with changes in goods and service prices, but not with prices for capital assets – bonds, stocks and real estate.

Such economic models all but ignore rent-seeking exploitation and the proverbial free lunch, yet real-world economics is all about obtaining a free lunch. That is why one seeks to become a political insider, after all. Yet such considerations are deemed to transcend the narrow boundaries of economics. These boundaries seem to have been narrowed precisely so as to limit the recognized "problems" only that limited part of economic life that can be mathematized, and indeed, mathematized without involving any changes in the social environment.

The resulting logical constructs of modern mathematical economics were not created without some degree of protest. Already a generation ago F. J. Dyson (1964:132f.) complained that "Mathematical intuition is more often conservative than revolutionary, more often hampering than liberating." Citing Ernst Mach's observation that "The power of mathematics rests on its evasion of all unnecessary thought and on its wonderful saving of mental operations," he worried that too much real-world complexity might be discarded.

Certainly the mathematical "badge of science" has distracted attention from the tendency for economies to veer out of balance.[3] The problem is that to achieve a single determinate, stable solution to any given problem (always posed as a "disturbance" to a pre-existing balance), general equilibrium theorists are driven to assume diminishing returns and diminishing marginal utility in order to "close the system." Such an approach is not a passive tool in the sense of an X-ray machine revealing the essential skeleton of reality. It is more a distorting mirror, in the sense that it formulates problems in a way that makes them appear amenable to being solved with a single determinate solution.

This singular solution is achieved by postulating a production function based on falling productivity as more labor is applied to capital and land. As for consumption, each added unit is assumed to give less and less satisfaction, so that more revenue is saved as economies become wealthier. This means a falling marginal utility of income: The more one earns, the less one feels a

---

[3] I discuss this problem in *Trade, Development and Foreign Debt: A History of Theories of Convergence and Polarization in the World Economy* (London: Pluto Press, 2 vols., 1993).

need to earn more. This is fortunate, because most models also assume diminishing returns to capital, which is assumed to be invested at falling profit rates as unemployment declines. Income and wealth thus are portrayed as tapering off, not as soaring and polarizing until a financial collapse point, ecological limit or other kind of crisis is reached. (It should be noted that the above variables all but ignore the economy's growing debt overhead relative to its assets, and the associated flow of interest.)

A particular kind of mathematical methodology thus has come to determine what is selected for study, recognizing only problems that have a single determinate mathematical solution reached by or what systems analysts call negative feedback. By contrast, a positive feedback model would depict an economic polarization that has an indeterminate number of possible resolutions as conflicting trends will intersect, forcing something to give. At such points the economic problem becomes essentially political. This is how the real world operates, but to analyze it would drive economists into an unstable universe in which the future is up for grabs. Such a body of study is deemed unscientific (or at least, uneconomic) precisely because it cannot be mathematized without becoming political.

The hypothetical "parallel universe" approach to economics

Marx (Capital, I:14) defined political economy's task as being "to lay bare the economic laws of motion of modern society." By contrast, equilibrium theory describes how market relations might settle at a stable resting point if only the world were something other than it is. An economic universe is envisioned that is not in political motion and that is not polarizing. This hypothetical world is characterized by automatic self-adjusting mechanisms, so that active government policies appear unnecessary. It is a world free of the financial dynamics of debt growing at compound rates of interest.

One must suspect a political reason for the aversion felt by economic model-builders to the real world's financial dynamics. To acknowledge their tendency to create structural problems would imply just what it did in Sumerian and Babylonian times: The desired economic balance must be restored by fiat, that is, from outside the economic system. Neglect of the debt overhead therefore is a prerequisite for economic models to generate laissez faire conclusions. A "what if" universe is postulated – the kind of world that might exist if finance capital were not a problem. After all, what is not quantified is less likely to be perceived and regulated.

Economies are supposed to be able to pay their debts simply by saving more. The working assumption is that saving is invested productively, not in creating yet new debts. Sufficient saving and investment thus are assumed to enable any society's growth in debt to proceed ad infinitum, as creditors are assumed to invest their earnings to further expand output and raise living standards. Any increase in saving is deemed to be good, regardless of whether it is invested productively or parasitically, physically or financially. Yet such saving in reality consists not only of direct investment in tangible capital formation. It also takes the form of stock market investment and real estate speculation in the ownership of assets already in existence, merely bidding up their price.

What is neglected is today's most characteristic pattern of lending: the investment of savings in the form of financial claims on wealth – bonds, mortgages and bank loans. Channeling savings in this way enlarges the volume of financial claims attached to existing productive assets in an exponentially expanding process. This debt overhead extracts interest charges which are recycled into yet new loans rather than financing new means of production to help economies "grow their way out of debt."

In recent decades such debt claims have grown more rapidly than tangible investment in factories and farms, buildings and homes, transport and power facilities, communications and other infrastructure. Economies have been obliged to pay their debts by cutting back new research, development and new physical reinvestment. This is the essence of IMF austerity plans, in which the currency is "stabilized" by further international borrowing on terms that destabilize the economy at large.

Cutbacks in long-term investment also are the product of corporate raids financed by high-interest junk bonds. The debts created by businesses, consumers and national economies cutting back their long-term direct investment leaves these entities even less able to carry their mounting debt burden. They are forced to live even more in the short run. Interest rates rise as debt-strapped economies become riskier, for as Adam Smith observed, "interest rates usually are highest in countries going fastest to ruin." And as interest rates rise, yet more money is shifted away from direct investment into lending at interest, until the system is torn apart from within. Capital flees abroad, the currency falls and unemployment rises.

No doubt a point must come at which the burden grows so large that it shakes the public out of its hope that matters somehow will return to normal. In the end the global economy must be obliged to do what Adam Smith said every debtor government historically was obliged to do: let its debts go. Now that global debts are becoming dollarized, however, it is less possible for a national economies simply to inflate their way out of debt so as to make what Smith called a "pretended payment." The only options are default or outright repudiation. But it has become academic fashion to imagine alternative "virtual realities" in which no such debt problems exist.

This turns economics into something akin to science fiction. The literary critic Colin Wilson has observed that in evaluating such fiction, the proper question to be asked is, what if the world were really like this? What does such speculation teach us?

Let us ask that question of today's monetarist fantasies. Fearing government regulation to be corrosive, monetarism warns that governments should not act to shape the economic environment. In particular they should not seek to regulate financial markets, for that would kill the goose that lays the golden eggs.

But is this Planet Earth, or a hypothetical world in which the charging of interest either was never invented, or was banned long ago? Such theorizing may be useful as an exercise in "alternative history" as it might have evolved in some parallel universe. But monetarist mathematics are not those of earthly reality. The economist's idea of science itself appears otherworldly. Not being amenable to a singular determinate mathematical solution, the problem of analyzing the incompatibility between the growth in debt claims and the economy's ability to pay is deemed unscientific. In this respect the way in which modern economists use mathematics diverges from what a scientific empirical economics would be.

The main criterion for success in modern economics is its ability to maintain internal consistency in the assumptions being made. As in science fiction, the trick is to convince readers to suspend their disbelief in these assumptions. The audience is asked to take seriously problems posed in terms of a universe in which money is spent on the production of current goods and services or saved, but not lent out to create a debt problem. Students are asked to believe that debts will not tend to grow beyond the means to pay, and that any disturbance in the economic balance will be met by automatic stabilizing responses rather than requiring action from outside the market economy. In sum, to believe that the growth in debt overhead is not a serious problem, it is necessary to suspend our natural disbelief in the fiction that shifting the money supply can steer interest rates to a precise level that will keep the economy's debt and credit, new saving and direct investment in balance.

Economics vs. the natural sciences: the methodology of "as if"

What is even more remarkable is the idea that economic assumptions need not have any relationship to reality at all. This attitude is largely responsible for having turned economics into a mock-science, and explains its rather odd use of mathematics. Typical of the modern attitude is the textbook Microeconomics (1964:5) by William Vickery, long-time chairman of Columbia University's economics department, 1992-93 president of the American Economic Association and winner of the 1997 Nobel Economics Prize. Prof. Vickery informs his students that "pure theory" need be nothing more than a string of tautologies:

> Economic theory proper, indeed, is nothing more than a system of logical relations between certain sets of assumptions and the conclusions derived from them. The propositions of economic theory are derived by logical reasoning from these assumptions in exactly the same way as the theorems of geometry are derived from the axioms upon which the system is built.
>
> The validity of a theory proper does not depend on the correspondence or lack of it between the assumptions of the

theory or its conclusions and observations in the real world. A theory as an internally consistent system is valid if the conclusions follow logically from its premises, and the fact that neither the premises nor the conclusions correspond to reality may show that the theory is not very useful, but does not invalidate it. In any pure theory, all propositions are essentially tautological, in the sense that the results are implicit in the assumptions made. [Italics added.]

This disdain for empirical validity is not found in the physical sciences. Ptolemaic astronomers were able to mathematize models of a solar system revolving around the earth rather than the sun. The phlogiston theory of combustion was logical and even internally consistent, as is astrology, former queen of the medieval sciences. But these theories no longer are taught, because they were seen to be built on erroneous assumptions. Why strive to be logically consistent if one's working hypotheses and axioms are misleading in the first place?

Lacking empirical testing and measurement, economics narrows into a mock-science of abstract assumptions without much regard as to whether its axioms are historically grounded. The self-congratulatory language used by economists euphemizes the resulting contrast between economics and science. "Pure" theorists are depicted as drawing "heroic" generalities, that is, banal simplicities presented in a mathematical mode called "elegant" rather than simply air-headed. To the extent that the discipline uses mathematics, the spirit is closer to numerology than to the natural sciences. Indeed, astrology also is highly technical and mathematical, and like economics it deals with forecasting. But its respectability has not lasted. Is this to be the destiny of today's economic orthodoxy?

At 1844 essay "On the Definition of Political Economy; and on the Method of first glance the sophistical tendency would appear to find an antecedent in John Stuart Mill's Investigation Proper to it":

> In the definition which we have attempted to frame of the science of Political Economy, we have characterized it as essentially an abstract science, and its method as the

method a priori. . . . Political Economy, therefore, reasons from assumed premises – from premises which might be totally without foundation in fact, and which are not pretended to be universally in accordance with it. The conclusions of Political Economy, consequently, like those of geometry, are only true, as the common phrase is, in the abstract; that is, they are only true under certain suppositions, in which none but general causes – causes common to the whole class of cases under consideration – are taken into account.

Mill's objective here was to isolate the principles appropriate to each dimension of social science, so as to avoid the confusion that resulted from intermixing them. Recognizing that people and societies were multidimensional, his logical method sought to segregate the various dimensions of social existence layer by layer, so as to deal separately with the economic pursuit of wealth, the political policy arena, and the respective subject matters of the other social sciences then emerging. This was not logic for its own sake, but for the sake of a systematic analysis proceeding step by step.

However, post-classical equilibrium economists have pursued logical consistency as an objective in itself. Disembodied from reference to how the real world operates, logic has been turned into a game. Rather than forecasting how the world will respond to the strains now building up, economists project existing trends in a political and social environment that is assumed to be unchanging. When this becomes a condition of the mathematical analysis itself, the idea of economics merely as "logical consistency" plays a much less logical role than it did in Mill's day.

The problems inherent in this approach are typified by Nobel Prizewinner Paul Samuelson's conclusion of his famous article on "The Gains from Trade" (1939:205 [1966 II: 782]): "In pointing out the consequences of a set of abstract assumptions, one need not be committed unduly as to the relation between reality and these assumptions." This attitude did not deter him from drawing policy conclusions affecting the material world in which real people live. He defended his Factor-Price Equalization Theorem (which states that under a regime of free trade, wages and profits will tend to equalize throughout the global economy) by claiming (1949:182) simply that:

> Our problem is . . . a purely logical one. Is 'If H, then inevitably C' a correct statement? The issue is not whether C (factor-price equalization) will actually hold; nor even whether H (the hypothesis) is a valid empirical generalization. It is whether C can fail to be true when H is assumed to be true. Being a logical question, it admits of only one answer, either the theorem is true or false.

Contrasting this theorem with the real-world tendency of international incomes and wages to polarize rather than equalize, Gerald Meier (1968:227) observes: "It need not . . . come with any surprise that factor returns have been so different . . . when in short, the restrictive conditions of the theorem have been so clearly violated in reality." But is it not sophistical to speak of reality violating a theory? Theory violates reality, not the other way around.

If one must be logical, why not start with realistic rather than merely hypothetical assumptions? The answer, I am afraid, is that realistic assumptions do not lead to the policy conclusions pre-selected by economic ideologues. This would explain why Samuelson-type trade theories continue to treat the international economy as a thermodynamic system to be analyzed by entropy theory, whereas the real-life world economy is an expanding system in which labor migrates and capital flows from low-income "cold" economies to high-income "hot" ones.

Wrong-headedness rarely is accidental; there usually is a self-interested policy motive. In his essay on "How Scientific are the Social Sciences?" Gunnar Myrdal (1956:336) observes: "Facts do not organize themselves into systematic knowledge, except from a point of view. This point of view amounts to a theory." He emphasizes that "contrary to widely held opinions, not only the practical conclusions form a scientific analysis, but this analysis itself depends necessarily on value premises."

What modern economics lacks is an epistemological dimension, the capacity for self-reflection so as to perceive the extent to which economic theorizing tends to be shaped by narrow self-interest. There is a bankers'-eye view of the world, as well as the perspective of financial manipulators, industrialists and so forth. It was the strength of Marxism to deal with economic theorizing critically on this level. Perceiving class biases, Marx viewed economic theory critically as apologetics for advocates of one policy or the other, a rhetorical system pleading for special interests. The 19th-century American protectionists likewise pointed to international biases between lead nations and latecomers regarding free trade theorizing. Today, a self-centered monetarist world view serves the global financial interests that have emerged to dominate the "real" economy. To understand its blind spots, an awareness of the self-serving motivations underlying Chicago School monetarism is necessary.

We are entitled to ask whose interests are served when economists claim that their assumptions need have no connection with reality, yet then proceed to make policy recommendations. Why do so many economics departments teach the assumptions of, say, the Heckscher-Ohlin-Samuelson theory of international equilibrium rather than starting from more realistic assumptions capable of explaining the real world's financial and economic polarization?

The products of low-wage economies exchange for those of better-paid labor for a number of reasons. Productivity differences have long been cited, but another factor also is at work: chronic depreciation of the currencies of low-wage countries as a result of the capital transfers they make in a vain attempt to service their foreign debts. In the end these debts will prove unpayable as they mount up at interest beyond the economic means to pay. The austerity programs used by the IMF and other creditor institutions are defended by models that conceal this mathematical inevitability. By depriving debtor economies of capital, educational programs and other basic infrastructure, austerity makes it harder for indebted countries to catch up. Matters are aggravated further by privatization programs that serve in effect as voluntary and self-imposed forfeitures of public assets to foreign and domestic creditors.

The use and abuse of mathematical economics

Creating a statistical profile of financial relationships is impaired by the fact that when wealthy individuals operate out of offshore banking centers, they appear nominally as "foreigners" in their own countries. Yet economists have constructed models in which such offshore havens, foreign debt, land values, and the composition of savings and debt appear as statistical black holes. Such omissions help these models serve as fairy tales to rationalize today's untenable status quo. Everyone is depicted as ending up in a stable and even equitable equilibrium.

A striking analogy of the impossibility of the world's financial savings continuing to grow at compound interest ad infinitum is pointed out by Edward O. Wilson, in Consilience (New York: 1998:313), citing "the arithmetical riddle of the lily pond. A lily pod is placed in a pond. Each day thereafter the pod and then all its descendants double. On the thirtieth day the pond is covered completely by lily pods, which can grow no more." He then asks, "On which day was the pond half full and half empty? The twenty-ninth day."

By the time people feel obliged to argue over whether the economic glass if half empty or half full, we are on the brink of the Last Days. To financial optimists, it may be pointed out that growth in the economy's savings is simultaneously growth its debt overhead. As debts grow, less and less saving is recycled into tangible direct investment. This may be good news for stock market and real estate speculators as savings are used to inflate the stock market and real estate bubble. But in the end the economy shrinks precisely because this "faux wealth" serves as a distraction, drawing savings away from direct investment in tangible capital formation.

What is lacking in the models preferred by vested interests is the use of mathematics to project the point at which trends intersect. At these crisis points economic forces do not have an inherently economic "solution," for the response must be political, by forcing a policy conclusion to be made.

A relevant mathematical economics would include an analysis of how wealth is turned into political power by campaign contributions, ownership of the popular press and media, and the subsidy of education and culture. These public relations for the vested interests promote "solutions" to crises that increasingly favor these interests as the economy polarizes. The analysis of such phenomena is dismissed by general equilibrium theorizing that assumes a constant and unchanging political environment. Changes in laws are deemed to be exogenous to the subject matter of economics proper. The word "exogenous" is heard so often these days (along with "externalities") that one wonders just what is left in economics proper. At issue for a more relevant empirical economics are the dynamics of social history, political institutions and the environment, not just the mechanics of supply and demand.

Governments tend to become the debtors of last resort. The culmination of this process is found in modern financial bailouts of private-sector ("socializing the losses" to savers). So we are brought back to Adam Smith's maxim that no government has ever repaid its debts. This is why nobody's savings have mounted up to become the equivalent of a solid sphere of gold extending from the sun out beyond the orbit of Saturn. The 12th-century accumulation of wealth of the Knights Templar was seized by Philip the Fair, who dissipated it in warfare. The wealth of the large Italian banking families subsequently was lost in loans to Britain's kings, who dissipated the proceeds in waging their perpetual wars with France. Most early debts were wiped out by wars, and by their inflationary aftermath in more recent times. Other fortunes were lost through confiscation, and bad judgment such as often is found with risky foreign investment. Some fortunes were dissipated by one's heirs or turned into land acquisition and other prestige asset ownership.

The relevant point for the social historian is that financial fortunes cannot continue to accumulate in the aggregate, precisely because the mathematics of compound interest are economically untenable. Throughout history it has become increasingly difficult to keep such fortunes viable. Money has been plowed back into increasingly risky new loans in ways that may impoverish and polarize the surrounding society to the extent that they find no counterpart in new tangible investment enhancing the economy's means to pay.

The moral of all this is that there are different kinds of mathematical economics. What the Cornell philosopher E. A. Burtt referred to the metaphysical foundation of modern physical science has become a politically tinged metaphysics in the hands of monetarists and neoclassical economists. Just how far their non-quantitative spirit diverges from the origins of economics is reflected in the closing words of David Hume's Enquiry Concerning Human Understanding:

> When we run over libraries, persuaded of these principles, what havoc must we make? If we take in our hand any volume; of divinity or school metaphysics, for instance; let us ask, Does it contain any abstract reasoning concerning quantity or number? No. Does it contain any experimental reasoning concerning matter of fact and existence? No. Commit it then to the flames: for it can contain nothing but sophistry and illusion.

Mathematizing the economy's monetary and financial dimension

Not all trends proceed at the same rate. At some point certain major trends must intersect, and something must give. This is the definition of a crisis – literally a crossing or intersection of trends where the political structure must accommodate itself to promote one trend or the other.

The example with which most people are familiar was made famous by Malthus, who argued that population growth tended mathematically to grow in excess of the economy's ability to supply food. The result, he concluded, must be starvation, wars or other "natural checks," or else a voluntary limit to population growth. Since the late 1960s the Club of Rome has warned that modern resource-consuming trends are unsustainable in light of the world's more limited growth in the supply of fuels and minerals, fresh water and air.

What these warnings achieved was to bring to peoples' attention the fact that whereas most mathematical economics has focused on foreseeable, narrowly determined consequences, over time the indirect "external" economies of commercial behavior tend to be larger than these direct economies. But they also have tended to evade mathematical and statistical treatment.[4]

The limits-to-growth warnings proved to be premature a generation ago, but one cannot say the same thing for the growth of debts/savings at compound interest year after year. Any statistician plotting the growth of an economy's debt quickly finds that existing trends are not sustainable. The growth of debt has become the major cause of economic downturns, austerity and financial polarization, creating financial crashes and, in severe cases, social crises.

Debt may be viewed as financial pollution, entailing major cleanup costs. Public policy is needed to cope with the incompatibility between the inability of consumers, businesses and governments to pay their stipulated debt service except by transferring an intolerable proportion of their assets to creditors. These transfers are done through bankruptcy proceedings, the liquidation of corporate or personal assets under distress conditions and (in the case of government debts) privatization selloffs.

The indicated solution is to limit the proliferation of debt by borrowing less, for instance, and to channel savings more into equities and tangible investment than into debt-claims on economic output. If present trends continue, it will be necessary to write off debts when they become too overgrown. This entails writing off the savings that have been invested in debt-securities – and this has now become the major political problem of our epoch. Yet monetarists – the very people who claim to specialize in financial science – see this crisis as an anomaly rather than a natural consequence of pursuing Chicago School policies. They urge economies to submit to financial austerity by sanctifying debts rather than saving themselves and their labor force at the expense of debt and savings trends.

---

[4] As early as 1849, Daniel Lee attempted to quantify the environmental depletion suffered by raw-materials exporters in his agricultural supplement to the U.S. Patent Office report. This "external" effect of foreign trade became an essential component of E. Peshine Smith's 1853 *Manual of Political Economy* (see Hudson 1975 for a discussion). Carey's Law of Association postulated that economies grow more productive at the intensive margin as they become more dense. But free traders have ignored these broad consequences, and used rhetorical invective censorially to dismiss them as "externalities."

An enormous volume of statistical research has been produced to analyze money and prices, and their links to interest rates and hence to the prices of bonds and other financial assets. When examining such research one should bear in mind that monetarism focuses on only part of the credit supply: bank deposits and "high-powered money" in the form of reserves invested in government debt. In reality the economy's entire range of securities and other assets is available to be monetized or, more literally, creditized. The potential credit supply consists of the volume of marketable securities and debts outstanding (which their holders can collateralize as the basis for yet more credit) plus equity in "real" assets, that is, the portion of tangible asset values to which debts have not yet been attached.

Most money and credit is spent on transactions in financial securities, not on "real" goods and services. Each day the equivalent of almost an entire year's national income passes through the New York Clearing House to buy stocks, bonds, mortgages and other bank loans. It thus is misleading to correlate the money supply only to transactions in current goods and services ("national product"). Such correlation analysis is not necessarily causal in any event. It is all too easy to mistake cause for effect. It therefore would be misleading to leave out of account the pricing of financial assets (bonds, stocks, and marketable debt securities such as mortgages, packaged consumer loans and so forth) and of the tangible assets (land and buildings, factories and equipment) on which this credit is spent. Nonetheless, these asset transactions seem to have disappeared from statistical sight as the focal point of monetarist analysis has shifted away from wealth and assets to consumer spending. For instance, despite the fact that the major asset for most families (at least in America and Britain) is the home in which they live, no adequate statistical time series for land and buildings is collected or published. In many cases one is obliged to estimate real estate values by looking at the growth of mortgage credit as a minimal proxy.

The very idea of what constitutes money remains in a state of confusion. To describe it simply as a set of counters neglects the fact that bank deposits and savings do not take the form of money as an abstract asset in itself, like gold or silver bullion. Rather, currency and bank money are debt/credit instruments. One person's saving usually finds its counterpart in other peoples' debts. If an individual or company deposits money in a bank or savings and loan association, a large portion of the deposit will be lent out as mortgage credit. Or, a saver may put money in a money market fund that channels its inflows into government bonds and corporate IOUs. The definition of "money" thus needs to be grounded in the overall superstructure of credit and debt.

An expanding superstructure of financial claims for payment grows and attaches itself to the economy's income and assets. These claims find their counterpart in liabilities on the opposite side of the financial system's balance sheet (e.g., the debts owed by the banks to their depositors, by insurance companies to their policy-holders, and so forth). They are securitized by the issue of bonds, mortgages and other IOUs. They represent the savings of people and the institutions through which people hold their savings, including pension fund contributions, Social Security, bank loan portfolios, insurance company reserves, and so forth. All these savings/debts must be paid out of future revenue.

Financial securities are not simply a mirror image of "real" economic activity, the "other" side of the balance sheet of assets and debts. They are a claim for payment that may be equal to, less than or greater than the economy's ability pay. When it comes to deciding what must give, the economy or its financial superstructure, the latter turns out to be more powerful – and hence, more "real" – than the economy's tangible flows of output and income. Entire economies are being crucified on the altar of debt and subjected to austerity and its foregone economic development. On this basis financial institutions have become the major economic planners of our epoch, usurping the former role of governments. Yet monetarists profess to oppose such centralized planning. What they evidently oppose is planning by elected officials with a broader set of social concerns than those of monetarist technocrats.

At the microeconomic financial level it seems wise to maximize one's return on equity by indulging in debt pyramiding. But for the economy as a whole this debt accumulates interest. Savings are lent out to finance this debt, as well as that of business and government. Wealthier economies tend to become the most highly indebted precisely because they have the most savings. Interest and amortization payments to savers tend to increase beyond the economy's overall ability to pay as debt service absorbs more and more personal disposable income and corporate cash flow. This constrains personal and business spending, creating the phenomenon of debt deflation. Yet no mathematical models depicting this process has been deemed acceptable by today's monetarist orthodoxy.

If there is any planning to be done with regard to the banking and financial system, the central issue of mathematical economics as applied to the financial sector should focus on how economies should cope with the tendency for debts to mount up until a crisis erupts? Monetarist models deny that any practical debt limit exists. Economies are supposed to "solve" their debt problem simply by succumbing to austerity, which is presented as the solution to the problem rather than a sign of having entered the financially moribund stage.

Perception of the debt-overhead problem is concealed by the characteristic feature of today's finance capitalism: an asset-price inflation of property markets, that is, rising land and stock market prices. This asset-price inflation goes hand in hand with debt deflation of the "real" goods-and-service producing economy. The failure to model this dichotomized economy is not the fault of mathematical economics as such, but reflects the constrained reasoning at the hands of the monetarist school that has monopolized economics departments in the world's universities.

Monetarist models serve largely to distract popular attention from the extent to which more wealth is being generated more by the asset-price inflation – than by building new factories to employ more people. What has happened is that the classical distinction between productive and unproductive credit has been replaced by an ostensibly value-free theory claiming that money earned in one way is just as economically worth while as money earned in any other way. This is supposed to be the case regardless of its consequences for employment, national prosperity or other effects held to be extraneous to purely financial concerns.

"Hard" facts tend to be the preoccupation of technocratic economics, whose predictions focus on the short run, that is, on marginal changes rather than structural transformations. But economic truth involves a much broader evaluation of society and even culture, as economic theory itself may be viewed as an exercise in cultural history. To the extent that "free market" monetarist economics has now become the world's de facto form of global planning, it threatens to bring about a poorer and more unfree world. If its models and their euphemisms do not make it clear just why this is the case, the reason is a politically motivated blind spot. Monetarist planning subjects the world to austerity to pay debts to a creditor class absorbing a growing proportion of the world's wealth, leading to economic polarization.

It is a world succumbing to economic collapse, heating up financially, ecologically and geographically to a critical mass. It also is heating up militarily as local provinces seek to secede from governments that are being turned into collection agents for global lenders. (Yugoslavia is the most notorious recent example.)

Trying to sell today's road to financial serfdom is much like trying to sell cigarettes. Popular fears of coughing, lung cancer, and other adverse effects are countered by advertising promises that cigarettes actually freshen the breath and are associated with vigorous outdoor life as epitomized by the Marlboro Man. Scientists are hired to provide a confusing flood of statistical analysis to dispute claims about smoking being causally associated with ill health, pretending that it is all just a coincidence. Neither the personal victims of smoking nor the public health agencies that must defray many of their medical costs are able to pierce the veil of such professionalized confusion.

In a similar way economists have been mobilized to serve creditor interests. Many of these hired guns act as public relations lobbies for global financial interests, often by joining think tanks that serve as advertising agencies to promote these interests. Their assigned task is to depict austerity as laying a sound foundation for future growth rather than promoting a self-feeding collapse. As poverty intensifies, governments are urged to bail out the economy's savers at taxpayer expense, cutting back wages even while shifting the tax burden from property onto labor. When the promised prosperity fails to materialize, the austerity lobby argues that the problem is simply that monetarist policies have not been followed intensively enough to "work their magic." But like most magic, the purported "magic of the marketplace" is merely a trick performed by model-builders so deftly that most peoples' eyes cannot quite follow what is happening.

As Eric Reinert has asked, if mathematical economics as practiced by the monetarists should face a product liability suit, what would be the appropriate judgment? If today's Chicago School orthodoxy were to be tested by reality, it would flunk the test. Jobs have been downsized. Lives have been shortened and the quality of life has declined as Chicago graduates and their clones have monopolized the staffs of national Finance Ministries, Treasury departments, central banks and the leading international financial institutions, using their positions to censor alternative economic analysis.

The crisis created between the economy's growth in debt and its ability to pay should be the starting point of mathematical economics.

Bibliography

Henry Adams (1919), The Degradation of the Democratic Dogma (New York).

Burtt, E. A. (1932), Metaphysical Foundations of Modern Science (London, 2nd ed.)

Hudson, Michael (1975), Economics and Technology in 19th-Century American Thought: The Neglected American Economists (New York).

Jordy, William H. (1952), Henry Adams: Scientific Historian (New Haven).

Marx, Capital, Vol. I (London, 1887)

Meier, Gerald (1968), The International Economics of Development; theory and policy (New York).

Mill, John Stuart (1844), Essays on Some Unsettled Questions in Political Economy (London).

Myrdal, Gunnar (1956), "How Scientific are the Social Sciences?" see An International Economy: Problems and Prospects (New York).

Nicholson, J. Shield (1893), Principles of Political Economy (London).

Samuelson, Paul (1939), "The Gains from International Trade," Canadian Journal of Economics and Political Science 5:195:205), repr. Papers, II:781-971.

Samuelson, Paul (1949), "International Factor-Price Equilibrium Once Again," Economic Journal 59:181-197 (repr. Papers, II:869-85).

Samuelson, Paul (1966), The Collected Scientific Papers of Paul A. Samuelson, ed. Joseph E. Stiglitz, Vol. II. (Cambridge, Mass.)

Vickery, William (1964), Microeconomics (New York).

Wilson, Edward O. (1998), Consilience (New York).

CHAPTER 7
U.S. "quantitative easing" is fracturing the global economy

> Moreover, it may well be asked whether we can take it for granted that a return to freedom of exchanges is really a question of time. Even if the reply were in the affirmative, it is safe to assume that after a period of freedom the regime of control will be restored as a result of the next economic crisis. Paul Einzig, *Exchange Control* (1934).[1]

Great structural changes in world trade and finance occur quickly – by quantum leaps, not by slow marginal accretions. The 1945-2010 era of relatively open trade, capital movements and foreign exchange markets is being destroyed by a predatory financial opportunism that is breaking the world economy into two spheres: a dollar sphere in which central banks in Europe, Japan and many OPEC and Third World countries hold their reserves the form of U.S. Treasury debt of declining foreign-exchange value; and a BRIC-centered sphere, led by China, India, Brazil and Russia, reaching out to include Turkey and Iran, most of Asia, and major raw materials exporters that are running trade surpluses.

What is reversing trends that seemed irreversible for the past 65 years is the manner in which the United States has dealt with its bad-debt crisis. The Federal Reserve and Treasury are seeking to inflate the economy out of debt with an explosion of bank liquidity and credit – which means yet more debt. This is occurring largely at other countries' expense, in a way that is flooding the global economy with electronic "keyboard" bank credit while the

---

[1] Paper presented at the Boeckler Foundation meetings in Berlin, October 30, 2010. I am indebted to Eric Janszen of i-tulip for bringing the Einzig quote to my attention.

U.S. balance-of-payments deficit widens and U.S. official debt soars beyond any foreseeable means to pay. The dollar's exchange rate is plunging, and U.S. money managers themselves are leading a capital flight out of the domestic economy to buy up foreign currencies and bonds, gold and other raw materials, stocks and entire companies with cheap dollar credit.

This outflow from the dollar is not the kind of capital that takes the form of tangible investment in plant and equipment, buildings, research and development. It is not a creation of assets as much as the creation of debt, and its multiplication by mirroring, credit insurance, default swaps and an array of computerized forward trades. The global financial system has decoupled from trade and investment, taking on a life of its own.

In fact, financial conquest is seeking today what military conquest did in times past: control of land and basic infrastructure, industry and mining, banking systems and even government finances to extract the economic surplus as interest and tollbooth-type economic rent charges. U.S. officials euphemize this policy as "quantitative easing." The Federal Reserve is flooding the banking system with so much liquidity that Treasury bills now yield less than 1%, and banks can draw freely on Fed credit. Japanese banks have seen yen borrowing rates fall to 0.25%.

This policy is based on the wrong-headed idea that if the Fed provides liquidity, banks will take the opportunity to lend out credit at a markup, "earning their way out of debt" – inflating the economy in the process. And when the Fed talks about "the economy," it means asset markets – above all for real estate, as some 80% of bank loans in the United States are mortgage loans.

One-third of U.S. real estate is now reported to be in negative equity, as market prices have fallen behind mortgage debts. This is bad news not only for homeowners but also for their bankers, as the collateral for their mortgage loans does not cover the principal. Homeowners are walking away from their homes, and the real estate market is so thoroughly plagued with a decade of deception and outright criminal fraud that property titles themselves are losing security. And despite FBI findings of financial fraud in over three-quarters of the packaged mortgages they have examined, the Obama Justice Department has not sent a single bankster to jail.

Instead, the financial crooks have been placed in charge– and they are using their power over government to promote their own predatory gains, having disabled U.S. public regulatory agencies and the criminal justice system to create a new kind of centrally planned economy in the hands of banks. As Joseph Stiglitz recently observed:

> In the years prior to the breaking of the bubble, the financial industry was engaged in predatory lending practices, deceptive practices. They were optimizing not in producing mortgages that were good for the American families but in maximizing fees and exploiting and predatory lending. Going and targeting the least educated, the Americans that were most easy to prey on.
>
> We've had this well documented. And there was the tip of the iceberg that even in those years the FBI was identifying fraud. When they see fraud, it's really fraud. But beneath that surface, there were practices that really should have been outlawed if they weren't illegal.
>
> … the banks used their political power to make sure they could get away with this [and] … that they could continue engaging in these kinds of predatory behaviors. … there's no principle. It's money. It's campaign contributions, lobbying, revolving door, all of those kinds of things.
>
> … it's like theft … A good example of that might be [former Countrywide CEO] Angelo Mozillo, who recently paid tens of millions of dollars in fines, a small fraction of what he actually earned, because he earned hundreds of millions.
>
> The system is designed to actually encourage that kind of thing, even with the fines. … we fine them, and what is the big lesson? Behave badly, and the government might take

5% or 10% of what you got in your ill-gotten gains, but you're still sitting home pretty with your several hundred million dollars that you have left over after paying fines that look very large by ordinary standards but look small compared to the amount that you've been able to cash in.

The fine is just a cost of doing business. It's like a parking fine. Sometimes you make a decision to park knowing that you might get a fine because going around the corner to the parking lot takes you too much time.

I think we ought to go do what we did in the S&L [crisis] and actually put many of these guys in prison. Absolutely. These are not just white-collar crimes or little accidents. There were victims. That's the point. There were victims all over the world. ... the financial sector really brought down the global economy and if you include all of that collateral damage, it's really already in the trillions of dollars.[2]

This victimization of the international financial system is a consequence of the U.S. Government's attempt to bail out the banks by re-inflating U.S. real estate, stock and bond markets at least to their former Bubble Economy levels. This is what U.S. economic policy and even its foreign policy is now all about, including de-criminalizing financial fraud. As Treasury Secretary Tim Geithner tried to defend this policy: "Americans were rightfully angry that the same firms that helped create the economic crisis got taxpayer support to keep their doors open. But the program was essential to averting a second Great Depression, stabilizing a collapsing financial system, protecting the savings of Americans [or more to the point, he means, their indebtedness] and restoring the flow of credit that is the oxygen of the economy."[3]

Other economists might find a more fitting analogy to be carbon dioxide and debt pollution. "Restoring the flow of credit" is a euphemism for keeping today's historically high debt levels in place, and indeed adding yet more

---

[2] "Stiglitz Calls for Jail Time for Corporate Crooks," DailyFinance: http://srph.it/aRwl4l, October 21, 2010.
[3] Tim Geithner, "Five Myths about Tarp," *Washington Post*, October 10, 2010.

debt ("credit") to enable home buyers, stock market investors and others to bid asset prices back up to rescue the banking system from the negative equity into which it has fallen. That is what Mr. Geithner means by "stabilizing a collapsing financial system" – bailing out banks and making all the counterparties of AIG's fatal financial gambles whole at 100 cents on the dollar.

The Fed theorizes that if it provides nearly free liquidity, banks will lend it out at a markup to "reflate" the economy. The "recovery" that is envisioned is one of new debt creation. This would rescue the biggest and most risk-taking banks from their negative equity, by pulling homeowners out of *theirs*. Housing prices could begin to soar again.

But the hoped-for new borrowing is not occurring. Instead of lending more – at least, lending at home – banks have been tightening their loan standards rather than lending more to U.S. homeowners, consumers and businesses since 2007. This has obliged debtors to start paying off the debts they earlier ran up. The U.S. saving rate has risen from zero three years ago to 3% today – mainly in the form of amortization to pay down credit-card debt, mortgage debt and other bank loans.

Instead of lending domestically, banks are sending the Fed's tsunami of credit abroad, flooding world currency markets with cheap U.S. "keyboard credit." The Fed's plan is like that of the Bank of Japan after its bubble burst in 1990: The hope is that lending to speculators will enable banks to earn their way out of debt. So U.S. banks are engaging in interest-rate arbitrage (the carry trade), currency speculation, commodity speculation (driving up food and mineral prices sharply this year), and buying into companies in Asia and raw materials exporters.

By forcing up targeted currencies, this dollar outflow into foreign exchange speculation and asset buy-outs is financial aggression. And to add insult to injury, Mr. Geithner is accusing China of "competitive non-appreciation." This is a term of invective for economies seeking to maintain currency stability. It makes about as much sense as to say "aggressive self-defense." China's interest, of course, is to avoid taking a loss on its dollar holdings and export contracts denominated in dollars (as valued in its own domestic renminbi).

Countries on the receiving end of this U.S. financial conquest ("restoring stability" is how U.S. officials characterize it) understandably are seeking to protect themselves. Ultimately, the only way this serious way to do this is to erect a wall of capital controls to block foreign speculators from deranging currency and financial markets.

Changing the international financial system is by no means easy. How much of alternative do countries have, Martin Wolf recently asked. "To put it crudely," he wrote:

> the US wants to inflate the rest of the world, while the latter is trying to deflate the US. The US must win, since it has infinite ammunition: there is no limit to the dollars the Federal Reserve can create.

What needs to be discussed is the terms of the world's surrender: the needed changes in nominal exchange rates and domestic policies around the world.[4]

Mr Wolf cites New York Federal Reserve chairman William C. Dudley to the effect that Quantitative Easing is primarily an attempt to deal with the mortgage crisis that capped a decade of bad loans and financial gambles. Economic recovery, the banker explained on October 1, 2010, "has been delayed because households have been paying down their debt – a process known as deleveraging." In his view, the U.S. economy cannot recover without a renewed debt leveraging to re-inflate the housing market.

By the "U.S. economy" and "recovery," to be sure, Mr. Dudley means his own constituency the banking system, and specifically the largest banks that gambled the most on the real estate bubble of 2003-08. He acknowledges that the bubble "was fueled by products and practices in the financial sector that led to a rapid and unsustainable buildup of leverage and an underpricing of risk during this period," and that household debt has risen "faster than income growth ... since the 1950s." But this debt explosion was justified by the "surge in home prices [that] pushed up the ratio of household net worth

---

[4] Martin Wolf, "Why America is going to win the global currency battle," *Financial Times*, October 13, 2010.

to disposable personal income to nearly 640 percent." Instead of saving, most Americans borrowed as much as they could to buy property they expected to rise in price. For really the first time in history an entire population sought to get rich by running to debt (to buy real estate, stocks and bonds), not by staying out of it.

But now that asset prices have plunged, people are left in debt. The problem is, what to do about it. Disagreeing with critics who "argue that the decline in the household debt-to-income ratio must go much further before the deleveraging process can be complete," or who even urge "that household debt-to-income ratios must fall back to the level of the 1980s," Mr. Dudley retorts that the economy must inflate its way out of the debt corner into which it has painted itself. "First, low and declining inflation makes it harder to accomplish needed balance sheet adjustments." In other words, credit (debt) is needed to bid real estate prices back up. A lower rather than higher inflation rate would mean "slower nominal income growth. Slower nominal income growth, in turn, means that less of the needed adjustment in household debt-to-income ratios will come from rising incomes. This puts more of the adjustment burden on paying down debt." And it is debt deflation that is plaguing the economy, so the problem is how to re-inflate (asset) prices.

(1) How much would the Fed have to purchase to have a given impact on the level of long-term interest rates and economic activity, and, (2) what constraints exist in terms of limits to balance-sheet expansion, and what are the costs involved that could impede efforts to meet the dual mandate now or in the future?[5]

On October 15, 2010, Fed Chairman Ben Bernanke explained that he wanted the Fed to encourage inflation – his of program of Quantitative Easing – and acknowledged that this would drive down the dollar against foreign currencies. Flooding the U.S. banking system with liquidity will lower

---

[5] William C. Dudley, "The Outlook, Policy Choices and Our Mandate," Remarks at the Society of American Business Editors and Writers Fall Conference, City University of New York, Graduate School of Journalism, New York City, October 1, 2010. http://www.zerohedge.com/article/why-imf-meetings-failed-and-coming-capital-controls.

interest rates, increasing the capitalization rate of real estate rents and corporate income. This will re-inflate asset prices – by creating yet more debt in the process of rescue banks from negative equity by pulling homeowners out of *their* negative equity. But internationally, this policy means that foreign central banks receive less than 1% on the international reserves they hold in Treasury securities – while U.S. investors are making much higher returns by borrowing "cheap dollars" to buy Australian, Asian and European government bonds, corporate securities, and speculating in foreign exchange and commodity markets.

Mr Bernanke proposes to solve this problem by injecting another $1 trillion of liquidity over the coming year, on top of the $2 trillion in new Federal Reserve credit already created during 2009-10. The pretense is that bailing Wall Street banks out of their losses is a precondition for reviving employment and consumer spending – as if the giveaway to the financial sector will get the economy moving again.

The working assumption is that if the Fed provides liquidity, banks will lend it out at a markup. At least this is the dream of bank loan officers. The Fed will help them keep the debt overhead in place, not write it down. But as noted above, the U.S. market is "loaned up." Borrowing by homeowners, businesses and individuals is shrinking. Unemployment is rising, stores are closing and the economy is succumbing to debt deflation. But most serious of all, the QE II program has a number of consequences that Federal Reserve policy makers have not acknowledged. For one thing, the banks have used the Federal Reserve and Treasury bailouts and liquidity to increase their profits and to continue paying high salaries and bonuses. What their lending is inflating are asset prices, not commodity prices (or output and employment). And asset-price inflation is increasing the power of property over living labor and production, elevating the FIRE sector further over the "real" economy.

These problems are topped by the international repercussions that Mr. Dudley referred to as the "limits to balance-of-payments expansion." Cheap electronic U.S. "keyboard credit" is going abroad as banks try to earn their way out of debt by financing arbitrage gambles, glutting currency markets while depreciating the U.S. dollar. So the upshot of the Fed trying save the banks from negative equity is to flood the global economy with a glut of U.S. dollar credit, destabilizing the global financial system.

Can foreign economies rescue the U.S. banking system?

The international economy's role is envisioned as a *deus ex machina* to rescue the economy. Foreign countries are to serve as markets for a resurgence of U.S. industrial exports (and at least arms sales are taking off to India and Saudi Arabia), and most of all as financial markets for U.S. banks and speculators to make money at the expense of foreign central banks trying to stabilize their currencies.

The Fed believes that debt levels can rise and become more solvent if U.S. employment increases by producing more exports. The way to achieve this is presumably to depreciate the dollar – the kind of "beggar-my-neighbor" policy that marked the 1930s. Devaluation will be achieved by flooding currency markets with dollars, providing the kind of zigzagging opportunities that are heaven-sent for computerized currency trading, short selling and kindred financial options.

Such speculation is a zero-sum game. Someone must lose. If Quantitative Easing is to help U.S. banks earn their way out of negative equity, by definition their gains must be at the expense of foreigners. This is what makes QE II is a form of financial aggression.

This is destructive of the global currency stability that is a precondition for stable long-term trade relationships. Its underlying assumptions also happen to be based on Junk Economics. For starters, it assumes that international prices are based on relative price levels for goods and services. But only about a third of U.S. wages are spent on commodities. Most is spent on payments to the finance, insurance and real estate (FIRE) sector and on taxes. Housing and debt service typically absorb 40% and 15% of wage income respectively. FICA Wage withholding for Social Security and Medicare taxes absorb 11%, and income and sales taxes another 15 to 20%. So before take-home pay is available for consumer spending on goods and services, these FIRE-sector charges make the cost of living so high as to render American industrial labor uncompetitive in world markets. No wonder the U.S. economy faces a chronic trade deficit!

The FIRE sector overhead has become structural, not merely a marginal problem. To restore its competitive industrial position, the United States would have to devalue by much more than the 40% that it did back in 1933. Trying to "inflate its way out of debt" may help bank balance sheets recover, but as long as the economy remains locked in debt deflation it will be unable to produce the traditional form of economic surplus needed for genuine recovery. A debt write-down would be preferable to the policy of keeping the debts on the books and distorting the U.S. economy with inflation – and engaging in financial aggression against foreign economies. The political problem, of course, is that the financial sector has taken control of U.S. economic planning – in its own self-interest, not that of the economy at large. A debt write-down would threaten the financial sector's creditor power over the economy.

So it is up to foreign economies to enable U.S. banks to earn their way out of negative equity. For starters, there is the carry trade based on interest-rate arbitrage – to borrow at 1%, lend at a higher interest rate, and pocket the margin (after hedging the currency shift). Most of this financial outflow is going to China and other Asian countries, and to raw materials exporters. Australia, for example, has been raising its interest rates in order to slow its own real estate bubble. Rather than slowing speculation in its large cities by fiscal policy – a land tax – its central bank is operating on the principle that a property is worth whatever a bank will lend against it. Raising interest rates to the present 4.5% reduces the capitalization rate for property rents – and hence shrinks the supply of mortgage credit that has been bidding up Australian property prices.

This interest-rate policy has two unfortunate side effects for Australia – but a free lunch for foreign speculators. First of all, high interest rates raise the cost of borrowing across the board for doing business and for consumer finances. Second – even more important for the present discussion – high rates attract foreign "hot money" as speculators borrow at low interest in the United States (or Japan, for that matter) and buy high-yielding Australian government bonds.

The effect is to increase the Australian dollar's exchange rate, which recently has achieved parity with the U.S. dollar. This upward valuation makes its industrial sector less competitive, and also squeezes profits in its mining sector. So on top of Australia's rising raw-materials exports, its policy to counter its real estate bubble is attracting foreign financial inflows, providing a free ride for international arbitrageurs. Over and above their interest-rate arbitrage gains is the foreign currency play – rising exchange rates in Australia and many Asian countries as the U.S. dollar glut swamps the ability of central banks to keep their exchange rates stable.

This foreign-currency play is where most of the speculative action is today as speculators watching these purchases have turned the currencies and bonds of other raw-materials exporters into speculative vehicles. This currency speculation is the most aggressive, predatory and destructive aspect of U.S. financial behavior. Its focus is now shifting to the major nation that has resisted U.S. attempts to force its currency up: China. The potentially largest prize for U.S. and foreign speculators would be an upward revaluation of its renminbi.

The House Ways and Means Committee recently insisted that China raise its exchange rate by the 20 percent that the Treasury and Federal Reserve have suggested. Suppose that China would obey this demand. This would mean a bonanza for U.S. speculators. A revaluation of this magnitude would enable them to put down 1% equity – say, $1 million to borrow $99 million – and buy Chinese renminbi forward. The revaluation being demanded would produce a 2000% profit of $20 million by turning the $100 million bet (and just $1 million "serious money") into $120 million. Banks can trade on much larger, nearly infinitely leveraged margins.

Can U.S. banks create enough electronic "keyboard credit" to buy up the whole world?

The Fed's QE II policy poses a logical question: Why can't U.S. credit buy out the entire world economy – all the real estate, companies and mineral rights yielding over 1%, with banks and their major customers pocketing the difference?

Under current arrangements the dollars being pumped into the global economy are recycled back into U.S. Treasury IOUs. When foreign sellers turn over their dollar receipts to their banks for domestic currency, these banks turn the payment over to the central bank – which then faces a Hobson's Choice: either to sell the dollars on the foreign exchange market (pushing up their currency against the dollar), or avoid doing this by buying more U.S. Treasury securities and thus keeping the dollar payment within the U.S. economy. Why can't this go on *ad infinitum*?

What makes these speculative capital inflows so unwelcome abroad is that they do not contribute to tangible capital formation or employment. Their effect is simply to push up foreign currencies against the dollar, threatening to price exporters out of global markets, disrupting domestic employment as well as trade patterns.

These financial gambles are setting today's exchange rates, not basic production costs. In terms of relative rates of return, foreign central banks earn 1% on their U.S. Treasury bonds, while U.S. investors buy up the world's assets. In effect, U.S. diplomats are demanding that other nations relinquish their trade surpluses, private savings and general economic surplus to U.S. investors, creditors, bankers, speculators, arbitrageurs and vulture funds in exchange for this 1% return on U.S. dollar reserves of depreciating value – and indeed, in amounts already far beyond the foreseeable ability of the U.S. economy to generate a balance-of-payments surplus to pay this debt to foreign governments.

The global economy is being turned into a tributary system, achieving what military conquest sought in times past. This turns out to be implicit in QE II. Arbitrageurs and speculators are swamping Asian and Third World currency markets with low-priced U.S. dollar credit to make predatory trading profits at the expense of foreign central banks trying to stabilize their exchange rates by selling their currency for dollar-denominated securities – under conditions where the United States and Canada are blocking reciprocal direct investment (*e.g.*, Potash Corp. of Saskatchewan in Canada and Unocal in the United States.).

The road to capital controls

Hardly by surprise, other countries are taking defensive measures against this speculation, and against "free credit" takeovers using inexpensive U.S. electronic "keyboard bank credit." For the past few decades they have stabilized their exchange rates by recycling dollar inflows and other foreign currency buildups into U.S. Treasury securities. The Bank of Japan, for instance, recently lowered its interest rate to just 0.1% in an attempt to induce its banks to lend back abroad the foreign exchange that is now coming in as its banks are being repaid on their own carry-trade loans. It also offset the repayment of past carry-trade loans extended by its own banks in yen by selling $60 billion of yen and buying U.S. Treasury securities, of which it now owns over $1 trillion.

Foreign economies are now taking more active steps to shape "the market" in which international speculation occurs. The most modest move is to impose a withholding tax on interest payments to foreign investors. Just before the IMF meetings on October 9-10, 2010, Brazil doubled the tax on foreign investment in its government bond to 4%. Thailand acted along similar lines a week later. It stopped exempting foreign investors from having to pay the 15% interest-withholding tax on their purchases of its government bonds. Finance Minister Korn Chatikavinij warned that more serious measures are likely if "excessive" speculative inflows keep pushing up the baht. "We need to consider the rationality of capital inflows, whether they are for speculative purposes and how much they generate volatility in the baht," he explained. But the currency continues to rise.

Such tax withholding discourages interest-rate arbitrage via the bond market, but leaves the foreign-currency play intact – and that is where the serious action is today. In the 1997 Asian Crisis, Malaysia blocked foreign purchases of its currency to prevent short-sellers from covering their bets by buying the ringgit at a lower price later, after having emptied out its central bank reserves. The blocks worked, and other countries are now reviewing how to impose such controls.

Longer-term institutional changes to more radically restructure the global financial system may include dual exchange rates such as were prevalent from the 1930 through the early 1960s, one (low and stable) for trade and at least one other (usually higher and more fluctuating) for capital movements. But the most decisive counter-strategy to U.S. QE II policy is to create a full-fledged BRIC-centered currency bloc that would minimize use of the dollar.

China has negotiated currency-swap agreements with Russia, India, Turkey and Nigeria. These swap agreements may require exchange-rate guarantees to make central-bank holders "whole" if a counterpart currency depreciates. But at least initially, these agreements are being used for bilateral trade. This saves exporters from having to hedge their payments through forward purchases on global exchange markets.

A BRIC-centered system would reverse the policy of open and unprotected capital markets put in place after World War II. This trend has been in the making since the BRIC countries met last year in Yekaterinburg, Russia, to discuss such an international payments system based on their own currencies rather than the dollar, sterling or euro. In September, China supported a Russian proposal to start direct trading using the yuan and the ruble rather than pricing their trade or taking payment in U.S. dollars or other foreign currencies. China then negotiated a similar deal with Brazil. And on the eve of the IMF meetings in Washington on Friday, Premier Wen stopped off in Istanbul to reach agreement with Turkish Prime Minister Erdogan to use their own currencies in a planned tripling Turkish-Chinese trade to $50 billion over the next five years, effectively excluding the dollar.

China cannot make its currency a world reserve currency, because it is not running a deficit and therefore cannot supply large sums of renminbi to other countries via trade. So it is negotiating currency-swap agreements with other countries, while using its enormous dollar reserves to buy up natural resources in Australia, Africa and South America.

This has reversed the dynamics that led speculators to gang up and cause the 1997 Asia crisis. At that time the great speculative play was against the "Asian Tigers." Speculators swamped their markets with sell orders, emptying out the central bank reserves of countries that tried (in vain) to keep their exchange rates stable in the face of enormous U.S. bank credit extended to George Soros and other hedge fund managers and the vulture funds that followed in their wake. The IMF and U.S. banks then stepped in and offered to "rescue" these economies if they agreed to sell off their best companies and resources to U.S. and European buyers.

This was a major reason why so many countries have tried to free themselves from the IMF and its neoliberal austerity programs, euphemized as "stabilization" plans rather than the economic poison of chronic dependency and instability programs. Left with only Turkey as a customer by 2008, the IMF was a seemingly anachronistic institution whose only hope for survival lay in future crises. So that of 2009-10 proved to be a godsend. At least the IMF found neoliberal Latvia and Greece willing to subject themselves to its precepts. Today its destructive financial austerity doctrine is applied mainly by Europe's "failed economies."

This has changed the equation between industrial-nation creditors and Third World debtors. Many dollar-strapped countries have been subject to repeated raids on their central banks – followed by IMF austerity programs that have shrunk their domestic markets and made them yet more dependent on imports and foreign investments, reduced to selling off their public infrastructure to raise the money to pay their debts. This has raised their cost of living and doing business, shrinking the economy all the more and creating new budget squeezes driving them even further into debt. But China's long-term trade and investment deals – to be paid in raw materials, denominated in renminbi rather than dollars – is alleviating their debt pressures to the point where currency traders are jumping on the bandwagon, pushing up their exchange rates. The major international economic question today is how such national economies can achieve greater stability by insulating themselves from these predatory financial movements.

Summary

The 1945-2010 world economic dynamic has ended, and a new international system is emerging – one that was not anticipated as recently as just five years ago.

Finance as warfare

From the 1960s through 1980s, the international economy was polarizing between indebted raw-materials producers in Africa, Latin America and large parts of Asia – "the South" – and the industrialized North, led by North America, Europe and Japan. Economists analyzing this polarization focused (1) on the terms of trade for raw materials as compared to industrial goods, (2) on the failure of World Bank programs to help "the South" cure its food dependency and other import dependency, and (3) on the failure of IMF austerity programs to stabilize the balance of payments. The IMF-World Bank model promoted austerity, low wage standards, trade dependency, and deepening foreign debt. It was applauded as a success story in the creditor-investor nations.

Today's world is dividing along quite different lines. The main actor is still "the North" composed of the United States and Europe. But the counterpart economic bloc that is emerging is growing less dependent and indebted. It is led by a rapidly growing China, India, Brazil and even Russia (the BRIC countries), joined by the strongest Middle Eastern economies (Turkey and potentially Iran) and Asian economies such as Korea, Taiwan, Malaysia and Singapore. This "BRIC bloc" and its allies are in payment surplus, not deficit. It is now the U.S. and European governments that find themselves debt-ridden beyond their ability to pay, especially when it comes to paying foreign governments, central banks and bondholders.

Yet the world is now seeing a race to convert electronic ("paper") credit creation from these already debt-ridden economies into asset ownership before governments in the payments-surplus economies to erect protective walls. Easy credit in the United States and Japan is fueling speculation in economies that are not so heavily loaded down with debt. This flight out of the U.S. dollar into Asian and Third World currencies is changing the global economy's orientation – in such a way as to restore financial dominance to nations running balance-of-payments surpluses, whose currencies promise to rise (or at least remain stable) rather than to fall along with the dollar.

As the U.S. and European domestic markets shrink in response to debt deflation, Asian countries and raw-materials exporters from Australia to Africa have recovered mainly because of China's growth. As in 1997, the problem they face is how to keep predatory U.S. and allied financial speculation at bay. This makes these countries the most likely to find capital controls attractive. But this time around, they are trying to keep speculators from buying into their assets and currencies, not selling them. Targeted economies are ones that are strong, not ones that are weak.

Since the mid-19th century, central banks raised interest rates to hold their currencies stable when trade moved into deficit. The universal aim was to gain financial reserves. In the 1930s, money and credit systems were still based on gold. Protective tariffs and trade subsidies aimed at running trade and balance-of-payments surpluses in order to gain financial reserves. But today's problem is too *much* liquidity, in the form of keyboard bank credit that can be created without limit.

This has turned the world of half a century ago upside-down. National economies in the United States, Japan leading nations are lowering their rates to 1% or less, encouraging capital outflows rather than payments surpluses, while their banks and investors are seeking to gain more by financial speculation than by trade.

Conclusion

The American economy may be viewed as a tragic drama. Its tragic flaw was planted and flowered in the 1980s: a combination of deregulation leading to financial fraud so deep as to turn the banking system into a predatory gang, while shifting the tax burden off real estate and the higher tax brackets onto wage earners and sales taxes. This increased the economy's cost of doing business in two ways. First, taxes on employees (including FICA withholding for Social Security and Medicare) and on business profits increase the cost of doing business for American industry.

Second, untaxing the site value of land (and most "capital gains" are actually land-value gains) has "freed" rental income to be pledged to banks for yet higher mortgage loans. This obliged new homebuyers to take on more and more debt as taxes were shifted off property. So homeowners working for a living did not really gain from low property taxes. What the tax collector relinquished ended up being paid to banks as interest on the loans that were bidding up housing prices, creating a real estate bubble. Meanwhile, governments had to make up the property-tax cuts by taxing employees and employers all the more. So the United States became a high-cost economy.

It didn't have to be this way – and that is the tragedy of the U.S. economy over the past thirty years. It was a fiscal and financial tragedy, with the tragic flaw being the propensity for the financial sector to engage in wholesale fraud and "junk economics." A flawed tax policy was endorsed by a failure of economic thought to explain the costs entailed in trying to get rich by running into debt. What Alan Greenspan famously called "wealth creation" during his tenure as Federal Reserve Chairman sponsoring asset-price inflation turned out simply to be debt leveraging – that is, debt creation when the dust settled and prices fell back into negative equity territory.

To rescue the increasingly irresponsible financial sector from its mortgage-debt gambles, the United States is taking a path that is losing its international position, ending the long epoch of what was actually a free lunch – the U.S. Treasury-bill standard of international finance. All that U.S. diplomats can do at this point is play for time, hoping to prolong the existing double standard favorable to the United States and its Treasury-debt a bit further, to permit U.S. bankers to get just one more year of enormous bonuses, in keeping with the American motto, "You only need to make a fortune once."

What no doubt will amaze to future historians is why the rest of the U.S. economy has let the banking sector get away with this! Apart from the Soviet Union's self-destruction in 1990-91, it is hard to find a similar blunder in economic diplomacy. It reflects the banking system's success in shifting economic planning out of the hands of government into those of finance-sector lobbyists.

U.S. officials always have waged American foreign trade and financial policy in reference to their own domestic economic interests without much regard for foreigners. The history of U.S. protective tariffs, dollar policy and interest-rate policy has been to look only at home. Other countries have had to raise interest rates when their balance of trade and payments move into deficit, above all, for military adventures. The United States alone is immune –

U.S. "quantitative easing" is fracturing the global economy

thanks to the legacy of the dollar being "as good as gold" during the decades when it was running a surplus.

To quote Joseph Stiglitz once again:

> [T]he irony is that money that was intended to rekindle the American economy is causing havoc all over the world. Those elsewhere in the world say, what the United States is trying to do is the twenty-first century version of 'beggar thy neighbor' policies that were part of the Great Depression: you strengthen yourself by hurting the others.[6]

It is natural enough for the United States to shape its international policy with regard to its own interests, to be sure. The self-interest principle is a foundation assumption of political theory as it is economic logic. What is less understandable is why other countries have not acted more effectively in their own interests – and why U.S. diplomats and economic officials should be so upset today when other nations in fact begin to do so.

---

[6] Joseph Stiglitz: "Foreclosure Moratorium, Government Stimulus Needed to Revive US Economy", *Democracy Now*, Oct. 21, 2010.

Lightning Source UK Ltd.
Milton Keynes UK
UKOW06f0034090316

269875UK00007B/317/P